Writing the Critical Essay

WEAPONS
OF MASS
DESTRUCTION

An **OPPOSING**  **VIEWPOINTS**® **Guide**

Lauri S. Friedman, *Book Editor*

Christine Nasso, *Publisher*
Elizabeth Des Chenes, *Managing Editor*

**OPPOSING
VIEWPOINTS**®
SERIES

GREENHAVEN PRESS
An imprint of Thomson Gale, a part of The Thomson Corporation

THOMSON
GALE

Detroit • New York • San Francisco • New Haven, Conn. • Waterville, Maine • London

THOMSON
★
GALE ™

© 2008 The Gale Group.

Star Logo is a trademark and Gale and Greenhaven Press are registered trademarks used herein under license.

For more information, contact
Greenhaven Press
27500 Drake Rd.
Farmington Hills, MI 48331-3535
Or you can visit our Internet site at http://www.gale.com

LIBRARY OF CONGRESS CATALOGING-IN-PUBLICATION DATA

Weapons of mass destruction / Lauri S. Friedman, Book Editor.
  p. cm. — (Writing the critical essay)
 Includes bibliographical references and index.
  ISBN-13: 978-0-7377-3860-5 (hardcover)
 1. Weapons of mass destruction. 2. National security--United States. I. Friedman, Lauri S.
  U793.W4264 2007
  358'.3—dc22

2007032863

ISBN-10: 0-7377-3860-X (hardcover)
Printed in the United States of America

CONTENTS

E xamining the state of writing and how it is taught in the United States was the official purpose of the National Commission on Writing in America's Schools and Colleges. The commission, made up of teachers, school administrators, business leaders, and college and university presidents, released its first report in 2003. "Despite the best efforts of many educators," commissioners argued, "writing has not received the full attention it deserves." Among the findings of the commission was that most fourth-grade students spent less than three hours a week writing, that three-quarters of high school seniors never receive a writing assignment in their history or social studies classes, and that more than 50 percent of first-year students in college have problems writing error-free papers. The commission called for a "cultural sea change" that would increase the emphasis on writing for both elementary and secondary schools. These conclusions have made some educators realize that writing must be emphasized in the curriculum. As colleges are demanding an ever-higher level of writing proficiency from incoming students, schools must respond by making students more competent writers. In response to these concerns, the SAT, an influential standardized test used for college admissions, required an essay for the first time in 2005.

Books in the Writing the Critical Essay: An Opposing Viewpoints Guide series use the patented Opposing Viewpoints format to help students learn to organize ideas and arguments and to write essays using common critical writing techniques. Each book in the series focuses on a particular type of essay writing—including expository, persuasive, descriptive, and narrative—that students learn while being taught both the five-paragraph essay as well as longer pieces of writing that have an opinionated focus. These guides include everything necessary to help students research, outline, draft, edit, and ultimately write successful essays across the curriculum, including essays for the SAT.

Using Opposing Viewpoints

This series is inspired by and builds upon Greenhaven Press's acclaimed Opposing Viewpoints series. As in the parent series, each book in the Writing the Critical Essay series focuses on a timely and controversial social issue that provides lots of opportunities for creating thought-provoking essays. The first section of each volume begins with a brief introductory essay that provides context for the opposing viewpoints that follow. These articles are chosen for their accessibility and clearly stated views. The thesis of each article is made explicit in the article's title and is accentuated by its pairing with an opposing or alternative view. These essays are both models of persuasive writing techniques and valuable research material that students can mine to write their own informed essays. Guided reading and discussion questions help lead students to key ideas and writing techniques presented in the selections.

The second section of each book begins with a preface discussing the format of the essays and examining characteristics of the featured essay type. Model five-paragraph and longer essays then demonstrate that essay type. The essays are annotated so that key writing elements and techniques are pointed out to the student. Sequential, step-by-step exercises help students construct and refine thesis statements; organize material into outlines; analyze and try out writing techniques; write transitions, introductions, and conclusions; and incorporate quotations and other researched material. Ultimately, students construct their own compositions using the designated essay type.

The third section of each volume provides additional research material and writing prompts to help the student. Additional facts about the topic of the book serve as a convenient source of supporting material for essays. Other features help students go beyond the book for their research. Like other Greenhaven Press books, each book in the Writing the Critical Essay series includes bibliographic listings of relevant periodical articles, books, Web sites, and organizations to contact.

Writing the Critical Essay: An Opposing Viewpoints Guide will help students master essay techniques that can be used in any discipline.

Weapons of Mass Destruction—The Threat From Past to Present

In 1961, the United States was in the thick of the Cold War with the Soviet Union. In this stand-off, each country was focused on intimidating and overcoming the other through the size and strength of their nuclear arsenals This tension came to a head on October 14, 1962, when U.S. spy planes captured images of Soviet nuclear installations in Cuba, just off the coast of Florida. The weapons were so close to the United States that the country was figuratively staring down the barrel of the nuclear gun. For 14 tense days the U.S. contemplated how to handle the nuclear threat just offshore. In the end, diplomacy prevailed; President Kennedy and then Soviet Premier Nikita Krushchev came to an agreement that resulted in the dismantling of both the nuclear installation in Cuba and U.S. installations in Europe that similarly threatened the Soviets.

Though disaster had been averted in what became known as the Cuban Missile Crisis, President Kennedy worried it marked only the beginning of a series of nuclear standoffs that would continually threaten life everywhere on the planet. Indeed, in addition to their own arsenals, the two superpowers helped allies in their relative spheres of influence to develop nuclear programs or to host their own nuclear weapons. This arrangement contributed to worldwide tension, as all over the globe countries served as pawns in the superpowers' nuclear game. President Kennedy feared this would one day result in a situation where the world's

A Soviet nuclear missile is destroyed in 1988. The build-up of nuclear weapons was a feature of the Cold War between the Soviet Union and the United States.

most dangerous weapons would become widespread and commonplace. In 1963 he remarked, "I am haunted by the feeling that by 1970, unless we are successful, there may be 10 nuclear powers instead of 4, and by 1975, 15 or 20.... I see the possibility in the 1970s of the President of the United States having to face a world in which 15 or 20 or 25 nations may have these weapons."[1]

[1] John F. Kennedy, The President's News Conference of March 21st, 1963. http://www.presidency.ucsb.edu/ws/index.php?pid = 9124

However, President Kennedy's worst fears did not materialize; in the year 2007, just nine nations are nuclear powers, and scores of others have relinquished weapons and abandoned weapons programs. Even nations formerly hostile to the United States, such as Libya, have been persuaded to give up their hand in the nuclear game for the global goal of reducing nuclear proliferation. Furthermore, there are just 16 countries with chemical weapons programs. It is thought that only between five and 12 have biological weapons programs.

Because of the relatively slow pace that nations worldwide have taken in adopting weapons of mass destruction, some experts view the threat they pose as being lower now than at any point in recent history. They argue that WMD proliferation, and specifically nuclear proliferation, is a serious yet stabilized issue that does not seriously threaten Americans or anyone else.

Some credit this success to the multi-decade international effort to reduce the spread of nuclear weapons, mainly through the Nuclear Non-Proliferation Treaty (NPT). The NPT prohibits signatories from developing weapons of mass destruction and prevents nations that are allowed to possess such technology from sharing it with others. South Africa, for example, in the 1990s dismantled its 6 nuclear weapons after signing the NPT. Similarly, Kazakhstan, Belarus, and Ukraine, each of which held Soviet nuclear weapons, relinquished their nuclear stocks upon signing the NPT. Other nations, such as Argentina, Australia, Brazil, Egypt, Japan, Libya, Spain, and many others have abandoned their pursuit of nuclear weapons in accordance with the Treaty. For military analyst William M. Arkin, this is evidence that "the threat of nuclear, biological, or chemical war has diminished to a lower level than at anytime in most of our lifetimes."[2]

2 William M. Arkin, "The Continuing Misuses of Fear," *Bulletin of Atomic Scientists,* Vol. 62, No. 5, September-October 2006, p. 42.

Several developments, in their opinion, indicate that the problem of nuclear proliferation is worse than ever. For example, the growing problem of terrorism, the number of unsecured nuclear weapons and fissile materials around the world, and the nuclear ambitions of rogue nations such as North Korea and Iran indicate to some that the problem of nuclear proliferation is getting worse, not better. According to political science professor David Cortright, the world has entered "an era in which the nuclear danger has become more diffuse and unpredictable.... The risk of a bomb actually exploding in a city somewhere is arguably greater now than during the Cold War and is likely to grow in the years ahead."[3]

Indeed, in 2003 North Korea withdrew from the NPT, and in 2006 successfully tested its first nuclear weapon to the dismay of the United States and its allies. The idea of nuclear weapons in the hands of the North Korean government headed by Kim Jong II, a notoriously unreasonable, paranoid, and megalomaniac ruler, upset many of America's foremost politicians, commentators, and military experts. Author Robert Galluci, for example, called the move "the most serious threat to [U.S.] national security."[4]

Furthermore, even though just nine nations have nuclear weapons, about 40 others are believed to have enough nuclear materials to build bombs or to jumpstart nuclear weapons programs. One such nation is Iran, a nation believed to have ties to terrorists and which is actively pursuing a nuclear program in defiance of international law. Said Senator Hillary Clinton in 2007, the reality that Iran could use nuclear weapons to hurt the U.S. and its allies adds "greater urgency to the necessity to doing everything we can to deny nuclear weapons to Iran. The regime's pro-terrorist, anti-American, anti-Israeli rhetoric only underscores the urgency of our response to the threat we face. United

[3] David Cortright, "The New Nuclear Danger: A Strategy of Selective Coercion is Fundamentally Flawed," *America*, December 11, 2006.
[4] Robert L. Gallucci, "Let's Make a Deal..." *Time*, October 23, 2006, p. 38.

States policy must be clear and unequivocal. We cannot, we should not, we must not, permit Iran to build or acquire nuclear weapons."[5]

Exploring whether the problem of weapons proliferation has worsened or improved since the Cold War is an important part of understanding the contemporary threat posed by such weapons and how to deal with the geopolitical issues they present. To this end, the articles and model essays included in *Writing the Critical Essay: An Opposing Viewpoints Guide: Weapons of Mass Destruction* expose readers to the basic arguments made about biological, chemical, and nuclear weapons, and help them develop tools to craft their own essays on the subject.

Whether or not the spread of nuclear weapons, such as this FGM-148B Javelin self-guided missile, is a serious threat remains a matter of heated debate.

[5] Senator Clinton's Remarks to the American Israel Public Affairs Committee (AIPAC) February 1, 2007, http://clinton.senate.gov/news/statements/details.cfm?id = 268474

Section One:
Opposing Viewpoints on Weapons of Mass Destruction

The United States Is in Danger of Being Attacked with Nuclear Weapons

William Perry

In the following viewpoint, William Perry argues that the risk of a nuclear attack on an American city is worse now than at any point during the Cold War, when the United States and the Soviet Union engaged in a nuclear standoff for decades. He discusses how nuclear weapons and fissile materials around the world are not adequately guarded, and thus are vulnerable to theft by terrorists. Furthermore, Perry warns that rogue nations such as Iran and North Korea seek to violate the Nuclear Non-Proliferation Treaty (NPT), an international treaty that prohibits non-nuclear nations from developing nuclear weapons, and prevents nations with the weapons from sharing the technology with others. The author warns that nuclear attacks on any American targets would be catastrophic, and urges lawmakers and international leaders to prevent the spread of nuclear weapons to terrorist groups and rogue nations before it is too late.

William Perry was the Secretary of Defense under President Clinton from 1994–1997. He also served in the Carter administration as undersecretary of defense for research and engineering, where he had responsibility for weapon systems procurement and research and development.

William Perry, "Post-Cold War U.S. Nuclear Strategy: A Search for Technical and Policy Common Ground," Remarks to the National Academy of Sciences, August 11, 2004.

I have been involved with nuclear weapons through my entire career. More than forty years ago I analyzed intelligence for President [John F.] Kennedy during the Cuban missile crisis [in 1961], when nuclear war seemed imminent. I worked on the development of new defense technology—stealth and smart weapons—during the mid-seventies, when it seemed that the Soviet Union might win the nuclear arms race. During that same period, I was awakened at three o'clock in the morning by the watch officer at NORAD [North American Aerospace Defense Command], telling me that his computers indicated that 200 missiles were on their way from the Soviet Union to the United States. Happily, that was a false alarm.

The Risk of a Nuclear Attack Is Worse Than Ever

I served as the Secretary of Defense during the mid-nineties, when Russia and Eastern Europe were in dangerous turmoil, and instituted a crash program to help them get

Former President Ronald Reagan and his advisors appear at a press conference to discuss the Strategic Defense Initiative (SDI, or "Star Wars") program, which proposed methods of shooting down nuclear missiles from space.

Americans Fear Being Attacked with Nuclear Weapons

The majority of the American public worries that if Iran develops nuclear weapons, it will either give them to terrorists to attack the United States, or use them to directly attack the U.S. and its allies. International polls show that on the whole, Americans believe Iran is more of a threat than Europeans, Asians, and Middle Easterners do.

	Give weapons to terrorists	Use them only defensively	- - - - - - - Attack - - - - - - -		
			Israel	U.S. or Europe	Muslim nations
United States	80	24	74	63	60
France	78	54	63	48	51
Germany	71	35	65	53	40
Great Britain	64	37	53	48	40
Spain	62	33	60	66	40
Russia	53	72	37	46	26
Turkey	36	55	51	48	29
Indonesia	23	80	49	50	11
Jordan	19	67	65	51	20
Egypt	17	57	61	43	15
Pakistan	7	55	13	19	9
Nigeria	49	37	45	55	15
Japan	52	25	43	36	39
India	33	43	35	36	24
China	29	55	31	34	20

Percent saying Iran is likely to:

Taken from: Pew Global Attitudes Project, "America's Image Slips, But Allies Share U.S. Concerns Over Iran, Hamas: No Global Warming in the U.S., China," June 13, 2006

their loose nukes under control. So I was close enough to the real dangers of the Cold War that the risk of a nuclear war never seemed academic to me.

But I have never, I have never been as worried as I am now that a nuclear bomb will be detonated in an American city. I fear that we are racing towards an unprecedented catastrophe. Unlike during the Cold War, the danger is not that another nuclear power will attack us. Deterrents remain powerful and compelling. The danger is that a transnational terror group will get their hands on a nuclear weapon and detonate it in a truck or a freighter in one of our cities, with disastrous consequences....

Steps To Reduce the Threat

The first imperative is to get the loose nukes problem under control. Using the momentum already achieved with the G-8 statements on nuclear terrorism, the United States should seek to establish a global initiative to place all fissile material, as well as the nuclear bombs, under strict control. Nuclear bombs, highly enriched uranium and plutonium should get the same protection as the gold that we guard at Fort Knox. The theft of a hundred kilograms of plutonium could have far more serious consequences than the theft of a hundred kilograms of gold.

The Nunn-Lugar programs [that reduce and guard nuclear stockpiles around the world] has made a good start on securing nuclear bombs and military fissile material and should be continued. But the fissile material used in commercial reactors is quite vulnerable to theft. It is effectively the weakest link and thus the one that a terror group is most likely to target. Senator [Richard] Lugar has recognized this problem and has proposed expanding the Nunn-Lugar program to deal with it. Inexplicably, his proposal is running into opposition in the Congress, and getting little support from the administration. Senator Lugar needs and deserves our support on this important initiative.

Soviet leader Mikhail Gorbachev (left) shakes hands with U.S. president Ronald Reagan during a 1987 White House ceremony. They have just agreed to a treaty to eliminate intermediate-range nuclear missiles.

But the United States cannot do this job alone. The moral support given by the G-8 was an important first step. At the next G-8 meeting the American President should put all of his weight behind persuading the G-8 nations to act on those initiatives. We need money, not just promises.

Prevent More From Joining the Nuclear Club

The second imperative is to prevent additional nations from going nuclear. As in dealing with the loose nukes problem, the proper vehicle is already established. In this case, the Nuclear Nonproliferation Treaty. But the NPT has loopholes that North Korea[1] and Iran are both exploiting. The solution to this problem is not to give up on the NPT, but to fix it. There are several proposals on how to do this, including an op-ed piece by myself, Brent Scowcroft, Arnold Kanter and Ash Carter, and the Carnegie Endowment has written perhaps the most thorough article on the subject. Without going into the important details discussed in these papers, their conclusion is that we can fix the NPT if we can muster the political will to do it. Basically, the nuclear nations have to agree to cut off support to any non-nuclear nation trying to establish a closed-fuel cycle. At the same time, the Security Council should establish that any nation that goes to the nuclear brink under the NPT and then withdraws from the NPT to go nuclear would face serious consequences. But whatever is done to fix the NPT, we are already confronted with an emergency situation with the ongoing proliferation of North Korea and Iran. We should put at the highest national priority the goal of keeping North Korea and Iran from developing a nuclear weapon production capability, and mobilize the other leading nations to join in a serious effort to prevent that disaster from occurring.

I am not suggesting that this will be easy, or that such a policy does not have risks. But if we fail to stop North Korea and Iran, the entire nonproliferation regime is likely to unravel....

The Cooperation of the Whole World Is Needed

All of the actions that I have proposed have two things in common. First, they are designed to greatly reduce the probability of a nuclear bomb being detonated in one of our cities. Second, they require deep cooperation from other nations, especially the other nuclear nations. All of these nations should share our objectives. The threat is to them as well as to us. But even so, the deep cooperation required will be

[1] In October 2006, North Korea developed nuclear weapons. It withdrew from the NPT in 2003 in order to do so.

hard to get. It will require real American leadership, and it will require America to demonstrate by its actions that it is serious about these objectives. At a minimum it will require the United States government to recommit itself to working with other nations to solve important problems in a spirit of international cooperation. And it will certainly require the United States to renounce its own development and testing of new nuclear weapons. We should be working, not only to reduce our nuclear weapons stockpile, but to clarify that our remaining stockpile is strictly for deterrence, not for war fighting.

I do not argue that nuclear weapons have no utility in war fighting, but I do argue that their relative utility is marginal in light of the dominant military position we hold today with our conventional military forces. And that the danger of a transnational terror group detonating a nuclear bomb in one of our cities far outweighs that marginal contribution. Only with a clear position of moral leadership in the nuclear field can we hope to lead the world in this critically important effort. And only by that leadership can we collectively take actions that prevent this nuclear catastrophe from occurring....

At Least Nine Cities at Risk

"Intelligence reports based on captured leaders and documents reveal that Al-Qaeda is targeting nine U.S. cities with the highest Jewish populations for attack .... The FBI has been monitoring radiation levels using CIA developed detection equipment (specifically designed to look for plutonium-based nuclear devices) at more than 100 mosques, homes, business and other sites in and around at least six of these cities."

Patrick Briley, "Hezbollah, WMD Attacks, Inside U.S. Cities?" *Newswithviews.com*, February 10, 2006. www.newswithviews.com/Briley/Patrick22.htm.

We Must Avoid Nuclear Annihilation

I will close by reminding you of what Andrei Sakharov wrote to my colleague, Sid Drell, during the Cold War: "Reducing the risk of annihilating humanity in a nuclear war carries an absolute priority over all other considerations."

And so it did, and so it does today. By giving that goal absolute priority during the Cold War we were able to avert the catastrophe then. We should do no less today.

Analyze the Essay:

1. Perry has served in several high level defense positions in the American government, including the Secretary of Defense. Does knowing his background influence the weight you give his argument? Why or why not?

2. William Perry claims that the threat of a nuclear attack is greater than at any point during the Cold War. How do you think William M. Arkin, author of the following viewpoint, might respond to this claim?

The United States Is Not in Danger of Being Attacked with Nuclear Weapons

William M. Arkin

In the following viewpoint, William M. Arkin argues that Americans should not worry that terrorists will attack them with nuclear weapons. Arkin claims there is no evidence to suggest that terrorists have acquired nuclear technology, and there is little reason why any nuclear state would help them do so. Arkin believes that officials push the threat of a nuclear weapons attack in order to perpetuate a state of fear and war and to bolster support for WMD programs. He concludes that while the idea of a nuclear weapons attack is indeed frightening, Americans are wasting their time worrying about something that is unlikely to happen.

William M. Arkin is a writer and commentator on homeland security. He hosts a blog called "Early Warning" on WashingtonPost.com, from which this viewpoint was taken.

Consider the Following Questions:

1. According to Arkin, what three events have been influenced by fear over nuclear weapons?
2. Why does Arkin discount the testimony of John Negroponte and Michael Maples?
3. What does the word "appetite" mean in the context of the viewpoint?

William M. Arkin, "WMD Terrorism is A Nightmare of Different Sort," Washingtonpost.com, March 2, 2006. Reproduced by permission of the author.

Terrorist "capabilities" to use weapons of mass destruction are "more limited" than those of states like North Korea and Iran, but the threat of terrorist attack with WMD is "more likely" than an attack by any state, top U.S. intelligence officials said [in March 2006].

Despite this broad assertion, U.S. officials offer only that there is the "possibility" of a future terrorist attack with WMD. They present no evidence that there is any actual terrorist capability, not a single example of terrorists receiving assistance from WMD states to develop their own capabilities, nor do they offer any intelligence indicators that terrorists are making headway towards achieving any WMD capability.

I've never thought that terrorists posed much of a weapons of mass destruction threat, and I've always thought that the specter of "nuclear terrorism" was promiscuous and politically motivated, both to undermine disarmament and to bolster U.S. WMD programs.

We Shouldn't Be Worrying About a Nuclear Attack

The image of a terrorist attack with weapons of mass destruction is certainly a powerful one, and the threat is so catastrophic, the Bush administration has made it a priority in fighting the war against terrorism.

It shouldn't be. What is more, there is also enormous cost in continuing to let the WMD nightmare rule: It was responsible for the war with Iraq; it was at the root of the failure of the Department of Homeland Security and FEMA to deal with hurricane Katrina; it is central to the current debate over the security of American ports.

Officials Exaggerate the Threat

Director of National Intelligence John D. Negroponte and Director of the Defense Intelligence Agency Lt. Gen. Michael Maples testified before the Senate Armed Services Committee [in March 2006] on the worldwide threats to the United States.

Their testimony was the usual combination of optimism about U.S. progress in the war on terrorism and happy talk about "encouraging developments in Iraq" together with dire talk about a dangerous and nightmarish world.

The "global jihadist threat," Negroponte said, is the "preeminent threat" to U. S. national security and interests abroad.

"The ongoing development of dangerous weapons and delivery systems constitutes the second major threat to the safety of our nation, our deployed troops, and our allies," Negroponte also said.

"We are most concerned about the threat and destabilizing effect of nuclear proliferation," Negroponte said, and "WMD-related proliferation and two states of particular concern, Iran and North Korea," is the central concern. But it is the terrorist threat with weapons of mass destruction that continue to get the administration excited.

The Probability of a Nuclear Attack is Very Low

"The probability of a terrorist attack with an actual nuclear weapon cannot be reliably estimated, and it is surely lower than the probability of virtually any other type of terrorist attack."

Veronique de Rugy, "Is Port Security Spending Making Us Safer?" American Enterprise Institute. Working Paper #115. Sept. 7, 2005. p. 8.

Everything Is a Weapon

Noting a time long ago "when a few states had monopolies over the most dangerous technologies," Negroponte said "al Qaeda remains interested in acquiring chemical, biological, radiological, and nuclear materials or weapons to attack the United States, US troops, and US interests worldwide."

"Indeed, today," Negroponte said, "we are more likely to see an attack from terrorists using weapons or agents of mass destruction than states, although terrorists' capabilities would be much more limited. In fact, intelligence reporting indicates that nearly 40 terrorist organizations, insurgencies, or cults have used, possessed, or expressed an interest in chemical, biological, radiological, or nuclear agents or weapons. Many are capable of conducting simple, small-scale attacks, such as poisonings, or using improvised chemical devices."

A South Korean military unit drives past a chemical attack drill near the border with North Korea.

Nuclear Stockpiles Continue to Decline

Global nuclear stockpiles are at an all-time low since the height of the Cold War. Russia has fewer than 16,000 total weapons (5830 operational) and the U.S. has fewer than 10,000 total weapons (5735 operational). Other countries – the U.K., France, China, Israel, India, Pakistan, and North Korea – have fewer than 1,000 combined.

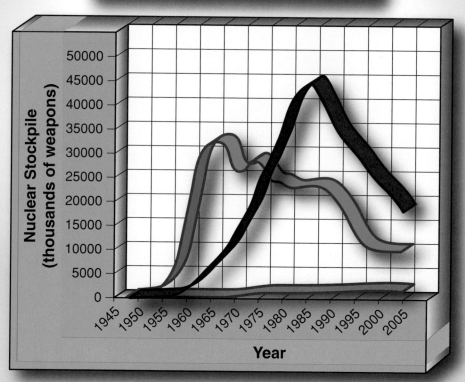

Taken from: Wm. Robert Johnston, www.johnstonsarchive.net

That's quite the arsenal. I guess in order to understand why U.S. officials would focus on terrorist weapons of mass destruction while IEDs and suicide bombers and civilian airliners seem quite effective, you'd have to understand the U.S. government's definition: Everything is a weapon of mass destruction.

The Threat Keeps the Bureaucracy Moving

And then there is the issue of proportion. North Korea's existing nuclear weapons, heck Russia's thousands of precariously controlled and maintained nuclear weapons, are less threatening than poisons or "improvised chemical devices" wielded by terrorists?

Neither Negroponte nor Maples offered any current intelligence indicating trends towards terrorists acquiring any of these capabilities.

"Several terrorist groups, particularly al Qaeda, remain interested in Chemical, Biological, Radiological and Nuclear (CBRN) weapons," Maples said. "Al Qaeda's stated intention to conduct an attack exceeding the destruction of 9/11 raises the possibility that future attacks may involve unconventional weapons."

Saying that nation-states were still "constrained by the logic of deterrence," Negroponte noted that such "constraints may be of little utility in preventing the use of mass effect weapons by rogue regimes or terrorist groups."

The truth is that the United States government has a gigantic weapons of mass destruction bureaucracy, from intelligence collectors and targeters to WMD scientists to the world's premier underground bunker physicists to "counter-proliferation" and "global strike" warriors to technology interdictors to effects analysts and disaster response cadres. There is no getting around the fact that that apparatus has both an appetite and an interest in characterizing the threat as worthy of enormous investment.

The basement of the Iraqi Ministry of Foreign Affairs after the U.S. invasion of Iraq. U.S. forces found that many records here had been destroyed, possibly to hide evidence of a weapons-of-mass-destruction program.

Too Scared to Think Straight

WMD are such an emotional threat that no one really asks whether the investment equals the threat or is focused on the right problem. U.S.-Russian nuclear disarmament is stalled and programs to safeguard existing WMD technologies and materials are starved in comparison with new programs to stop "proliferation" (read terrorist proliferation).

All based on bureaucratic self-justification and someone's unsubstantiated nightmare?

Analyze the Essay:

1. In his essay, William M. Arkin claims there are political reasons why leaders insist that Americans are vulnerable to a nuclear weapons attack. What is your assessment of this claim? Examine the political events Arkin claims have been influenced by fear of a nuclear weapons attack and state your opinion on whether they were valid or invalid fears.

2. In his conclusion, Arkin calls a nuclear attack an "emotional threat". Explain what you think Arkin means by this term and whether you agree.

The United States Is in Danger of Being Attacked with Biochemical Weapons

Bill Frist

In the following viewpoint, former Senator Bill Frist warns the threat of a biochemical weapons attack against America is real and must be guarded against. Frist discusses why biochemical weapons pose such a dangerous threat: they are easily dispersible, hard to detect, and cheap and easy to manufacture by terrorists. Worse, says Frist, the United States's vaccine stocks and hospital facilities are woefully unprepared for such an attack. If terrorists were to launch a biochemical attack on the United States, Frist predicts it would make the attacks of September 11th look like a minor accident. For this reason, Frist proposes beginning a Manhattan Project—the project that resulted in the development of the first nuclear weapon that helped the United States win World War II—to thwart biochemical attacks. Only in this way can the United States avoid disaster, concludes Frist.

Bill Frist was a U.S. Senator from Tennessee from 1995 to 2007, and is also a doctor of medicine.

Consider the Following Questions:

1. According to the author, how many people could be killed in a biochemical terrorist attack?
2. What is H5N1, according to the author, and what bearing does it have on his argument?
3. Why is a biological attack on "one country an attack upon all," according to Frist?

Bill Frist, "The Manhattan Project for the 21st Century," Nantucket, Massachusetts, August 3, 2005.

Like everyone else, politicians tend to look away from danger, to hope for the best, and pray that disaster will not arrive on their watch even as they sleep through it. This is so much a part of human nature that it often goes unchallenged.

But we will not be able to sleep through what is likely coming soon—a front of unchecked and virulent epidemics, the potential of which should rise above your every other concern. For what the world now faces, it has not seen even in the most harrowing episodes of the Middle Ages or the great wars of the last century....

Far Worse than September 11th

To see what might lie on the horizon one need only look to the relatively recent past. I have a photograph of an emergency hospital in Kansas during the 1918 influenza pandemic. People lie miserably on cots in an enormous barn-like room with beams of sunlight streaming through high windows. It seems more crowded than the main floor of Grand Central Station at five o'clock on a weekday. In this one room several hundred people are in the throes of distress.

Think of two thousand such rooms filled with a crush of men, women, and children—500,000 in all—and imagine that the shafts of sunlight that illuminate them for us almost a century later are the last light they will ever see. Then bury them. That is what happened. How would a nation so greatly moved and touched by the 3,000 dead of September 11th react to half a million dead?

> ## Biochemical Weapons are the Greatest Threat We Face
>
> "A lone individual with a modicum of microbiology laboratory training, and with access to a select agent, could produce a biological arsenal in a few weeks. ... Blocking their acquisition is a formidable challenge."
>
> Leonard A. Cole, "Bioweapons, Proliferation, and the U.S. Anthrax Attack," Center for Contemporary Conflict, www.ccc.nps.navy.mil//events/recent/Presentations/Cole%20Bio%20paper.pdf.

Vials containing agents that could be used to produce biological weapons, recovered from the residence of an Iraqi scientist in 2003. U.S. forces believe the vials were being kept as "seed stock" in case Saddam Hussein decided to restart his biological weapons program.

In 1918–1919 the mortality rate was 3 percent, which seems merciful in comparison to the 50 percent mortality rate of today's highly pathogenic H5N1 avian flu. In just the last 18 months, avian flu has caused the death or destruction of over 140 million birds in 11 Asian nations. And, most alarmingly, in 4 of those nations, H5N1 has taken the worried jump from birds to infect humans.

Should the virus shift and human-to-human transmission become sustained, imagine how many human lives avian flu will take. How then would a nation greatly moved and touched by three thousand dead, react to 5 or 50 million dead?

Terrorists Could Cause the Deaths of Millions

The new realities of terrorism and suicide bombers pull us one step further. How would we react to the devastation caused by a virus or bacteria or other pathogen unleashed not by the forces of nature, but intentionally by man?

During the Cold War, the Soviet Union, which stockpiled 5,000 tons annually of biowarfare-engineered anthrax resistant to 16 antibiotics, also produced massive amounts of weaponized smallpox—just as the monumental effort to immunize the world's children came to a successful close.

It is impossible to rule out that quantities of this or other deliberately manufactured pathogens such as pneumonic plague, tularemia, or botulinum toxin may find or may have found their ways into the possession of terrorists such as [Osama] bin Laden and [Abu Musabal-] Zarqawi [terrorist leader in Iraq who was killed in 2006 by U.S. military forces].

We Are Dangerously Unprepared for a Biochem Attack

Although the United States now has enough smallpox vaccine for the entire population, we have neither the means of distribution nor the immunized personnel to administer it

Biochemical Weapons: How They Kill

There are many biological and chemical agents that can be weaponized.
They vary in their symptoms and effects on the body.

BIOLOGICAL TOXINS

Toxin	Symptoms	Effects if untreated
Aflatoxin	Headache, jaundice, gastrointestinal distress	Liver disease, internal bleeding, possible death
Anthrax	Fever, malaise, cough, respiratory distress	Shock and death within 36 hours of severe symptoms
Botulinum toxins	Weakness, dizziness, dry throat, blurred vision, problems speaking and hearing, difficulty swallowing	Paralysis, respiratory failure, death
Bubonic plague	Malaise, high fever, tender lymph nodes	Blood poisoning, death
Cholera	Vomiting, abdominal distension, pain, diarrhea	Severe dehydration, shock, death
Pneumonic plague	High fever, chills, headache, coughing up blood, blood poisoning	Respiratory failure, circulatory collapse, heavy bleeding, death
Q fever	Fever, cough, chest pain	Generally not fatal
Ricin	Weakness, fever, cough, hypothermia	Dangerously low blood pressure, heart failure, death
Smallpox	Malaise, fever, vomiting, headache, backache, blister-like rash	Bone marrow depression, bleeding, death
Staphylococcal enterotoxin B	Fever, chills, headache, muscle aches, cough	Septic shock, death
Tularemia	Swollen glands, fever, headache, malaise, weight loss, nonproductive cough	Generally not fatal
Viral hemorrhagic fevers	Easy bleeding, red spots on skin, low blood pressure, flushed face and chest, swelling of ankles and other joints	Uncontrollable bleeding, circulatory collapse, death

CHEMICAL TOXINS

Toxin	Symptoms	Effects if untreated
Nerve agents, including VX, GB and GD	Runny nose, tightness of chest, dim vision, pinpointing of eye pupils, difficulty breathing, drooling, excessive sweating. Nausea, vomiting, cramps, involuntary urination and defecation, jerking, staggering, headache, confusion, drowsiness	Convulsions, coma, cessation of breathing, death
Sulfur Mustard Agent	Eye irritation, skin blemishes and blisters, inflammation of the nose, throat and lung, malaise, vomiting, fever. Classified as a carcinogen.	Blocks cell growth, suppresses bone marrow

Taken from: U.S. Army Medical Research Institute of Infectious Diseases,
U.S. Army Center for Health Promotion and Preventive Medicine

in a generalized outbreak nor the certainty that the vaccine we have would even be relevant to a specific weaponized strain of the virus.

Hospitals and our long neglected public health infrastructure would be quickly overwhelmed. Panic, suffering, and the spread of the disease would intensify as—because people were dead, sick, or afraid—the economy ceased to function, electrical power flickered out, and food and medical supplies failed to move.

Over months or perhaps years, scores of millions might perish, with whole families dying in their houses and no one to memorialize them or remove their corpses. Almost without doubt, the epidemic would spread to the rest of the world, for in biological warfare an attack upon one country is an attack upon all.

Every vestige of modernity would be overturned. The continual and illusory flirtation with immortality that is a hallmark of our scientific civilization would shatter. And we would find ourselves looking back upon even the most difficult times of the last century as a golden age....

Terrorists Could Create Apocalyptic Weapons

No intelligence agency, no matter how astute, and no military, no matter how powerful and dedicated, can assure that a few technicians of middling skill using a few thousand dollars worth of readily available equipment in a small and apparently innocuous setting cannot mount a first-order biological attack.

It's possible today to synthesize virulent pathogens from scratch, or to engineer and manufacture prions that, introduced undetectably over time into a nation's food supply, would after a long delay afflict millions with a terrible and often fatal disease. It's a new world.

Unfortunately, the permutations are so various that the research establishment as now constituted cannot set up lines of investigation to anticipate even a small proportion of them. But is it really reasonable to assume that anyone might resort to biological warfare? Indeed it is.

Though Al-Qaida's leadership has been decimated, it has declared that, "We have the right to kill four million Americans—two million of them children .... [and] it is our right to fight them with chemical and biological weapons."

Humanity's Most Important Battle

It's hardly necessary, however, to rely upon stated intent. One need only weigh the logic of terrorism, its evolution, its absolutist convictions, and the evidence in documents and materials found in terrorist redoubts.

Though not as initially dramatic as a nuclear blast, biological warfare is potentially far more destructive than the kind of nuclear attack feasible at the operational level of the terrorist. And biological war is itself distressingly easy to wage.

Never have we had to fight such a battle, to protect so many people against so many threats that are so silent and so lethal.

A Call to Action

So what must we do? I propose an unprecedented effort—a "Manhattan Project for the 21st Century"—not with the goal of creating a destructive new weapon, but to defend against destruction wreaked by infectious disease and biological weapons.

I speak of substantial increases in support for fundamental research, medical education, emergency capacity, and public health infrastructure. I speak of an unleashing of the private sector and unprecedented collaboration between government and industry and academia. I speak of the

creation of secure stores of treatments and vaccines and vast networks of distribution.

Above all, I speak not of the creation of a forest of bureaucratic organization charts and the repetition of a hundred million Latinate words in a hundred million meetings that substitute for action, but action itself—without excuses, without exceptions—with the goal of protecting every American and the capability to help protect the people of the world.

The Al Hakam biological weapons plant in Iraq as it is destroyed by the United Nations, in 1996.

I call for the creation of the ability to detect, identify, and model any emerging or newly emerging infection, present or future, natural or otherwise—for the ability to engineer the immunization and cure, and to manufacture, distribute, and administer what we need to get it done and to get it done in time.

Our Survival Depends on Preventing a Biochemical Attack

This is a bold vision. But it is the kind of thing that, once accomplished, is done. And it is the kind of thing that calls out to be done—and that, if not done, will indict us forever in the eyes of history.

In diverting a portion of our vast resources to protect nothing less than our lives, the lives of our children, and the life of our civilization, many benefits other than survival would follow in train—not least the satisfaction of having done right.

Analyze the Essay:

1. The author concludes his essay by making suggestions for how the U.S. might improve its response to the threat of a biochemical attack. What are these suggestions? Do you think they can help mitigate the threat posed by biochemical weapons? Why or why not?

2. To make his argument that biochemical weapons pose a serious threat to Americans, Frist paints a picture of what society would look like after being hit with weaponized biological pathogens. What details and images does he use to paint this picture? What descriptions are particularly striking, in your opinion?

The United States Is Not in Danger of Being Attacked with Biochemical Weapons

Viewpoint
Four

Allison Macfarlane

In the following viewpoint, author Allison Macfarlane casts doubt on the idea that the United States faces a serious threat from biochemical weapons. Though such an attack would likely be devastating, Macfarlane argues there is very little evidence to show that terrorists are actually able to acquire such weapons, or even to carry out a successful attack. Macfarlane states that biochemical pathogens are very difficult to use as a lethal weapon because of their unreliability. She cites historical examples in which biochemical pathogens were released but only killed a handful of people, if any. Macfarlane concludes that terrorists probably don't have the expertise to make such weapons actually work and thus they are not likely to be used in an attack against the United States.

   Allison M. Macfarlane is a research associate in the Science, Technology, and Global Security Working Group in MIT's Program in Science, Technology, and Society.

Consider the Following Questions:
1. What does the word "weaponize" mean in the context of the viewpoint?
2. What was the outcome of the 1993 Aum Shinrikyo anthrax attack, according to Macfarlane?
3. What constitutes a larger threat to the United States than biochemical weapons, in Macfarlane's opinion?

Allison Macfarlane, "Assessing the Threat," *Technology Review*, March–April 2006, p. 34. © 2006 by the Association of Alumni and Alumnae of MIT. Reproduced by permission.

Could terrorists, intent on causing as much harm and societal disruption as possible, use new biotechnology processes to engineer a virulent pathogen that, when unleashed, would result in massive numbers of dead? [*Technology Review* author] Mark Williams, in his article "The Knowledge," suggests we should be contemplating this doomsday scenario in the 21st century. Williams's article might make you sleep less soundly, but are the threats real? The truth is that we do not really know.

Biochemical Weapons Are Hard to Make

Part of the problem is that even if terrorists could create new pathogens virulent to humans, it's not at all clear that they could "weaponize" them—that is, put the pathogens into a form that is highly infectious to humans and then disperse them in ways that expose large numbers of people.

Past experience suggests that this is not an easy task. During World War II, the Japanese dropped plague-infected materials on Chinese cities, to limited effect. In 1979, the Soviets caused 66 deaths from anthrax by accidentally releasing it from a bioweapons facility in Sverdlovsk. In 1984, the Rajneeshees cult contaminated salad bars in the Dalles, OR, with salmonella, but their actions killed no one. In 1993, the Aum Shinrikyo cult failed to kill anyone after carrying out multiple attacks with anthrax in Japan. Finally, the 2001 anthrax letter attacks in the U.S. killed five people. These were all frightening events. They were not, however, grave threats to national security.

Inaccurate and Unclear Data

Yet estimates of bioweapons dangers tend to be dire, like those in Williams's article. The truth is that the data are too thin to make accurate projections of the effects of bioweapons attacks. I surveyed seven separate estimates of fatalities from a projected anthrax attack. The lowest estimate, by

A soldier in the South Carolina National Guard's 43rd Weapons of Mass Destruction Civil Support Team demonstrates his protective gear. His unit is certified to respond to WMD emergencies.

Milton Leitenberg, ranged from zero to 1,440 dead per kilogram of anthrax used, while the highest, by Lawrence Wein and others, put fatalities between 123,400 and 660,000 per kilogram of anthrax. Most of these estimates were made on the basis of little actual data.

To predict accurately the effects of bioweapons, data are needed on the amount of agent required to infect a person, the percentage of people who survive an infection (which depends on the health of the population), the transmission rate if the agent is contagious, the ability to aerosolize and disperse an agent effectively (which depends, in turn, on climatic conditions), the environmental stability of an agent,

An Attack Using Biochemical Weapons Is Not Likely

Political, military, and scientific experts polled by *Foreign Policy* magazine believe that a terrorist attack is not likely to come in the form of a biological or chemical attack.

Regardless of what you think about the timing of an attack, what two methods are most likely to be used in America by global terrorists?	
Respondents who selected...	Percent
Suicide bombing attack	67
Attack on major infrastructure	66
Attack using radiological weapon	20
Cyberattack	12
Attack on chemical or nuclear plants	11
Chemical weapon attack	10
Biological weapon attack	9
Nuclear weapon attack	6

Taken from: *Foreign Policy*, "The Terrorism Index," July–August 2006.

The Israel Institute for Biological Research, believed to be responsible for producing chemical and biological weapons for Israel's military.

the population density, and the abilities of the public-health system, including when an attack is detected and whether prophylactics, vaccines, or antidotes exist and, if so, in what quantities.

It Is Uncertain That Terrorists Would Be Able to Weaponize Pathogens

For any one pathogen—even one familiar to us, like small-pox and anthrax—not all of these variables are known, and therefore quantitative predictions are not possible with a high degree of certainty. In the words of the U.S. National Academy of Sciences in a 2002 report, "these factors produce an irreducible uncertainty of several orders of magnitude in the number of people who will be infected in an open-air release."

For example, data on the infectiousness of an agent varies widely, depending on the agent. Because of limited experience with anthrax, susceptibility data have often been extrapolated from animal trials that have little bearing on human response to agents. In the case of smallpox, with which scientists had much experience in the 20th century, some factors remain uncertain, such as the transmission rate.

In the models of bioweapons attacks, the ability to weaponize an agent and disperse it effectively is estimated in part from open-air trials done by the U.S. Army between the 1940s and 1960s. These trials used live simulants of agents on major U.S. cities, but the behavior of a real bioweapon

---

We Have Bigger Problems than the Threat from Biochemical Weapons

"Bioterrorism may or may not develop into a serious concern in the future, but it is not 'one of the most pressing problems that we have on the planet today.'"

Milton Leitenberg, "Assessing the Biological Weapons and Bioterrorism Threat," *Strategic Studies Institute*, December 2005, p. 87.

agent in such a situation remains uncertain. Williams's article doesn't describe in any detail the ability of terrorists to weaponize any of the theorized agents. Yet making effective bioweapons would take a tremendous amount of work.

Give Other Defense Programs Priority

While a state-sponsored program might have the means to do that work, terrorist groups probably don't. With so much uncertainty surrounding the outcome of a bioweapons attack, it does not make sense to plan extensive biodefense programs when more-certain threats, particularly those involving nuclear weapons, require attention.

Analyze the Essay:

1. What experts does Macfarlane quote in her essay? In what way does she use the quotes?
2. Authors Allison Macfarlane and Bill Frist disagree on whether biochemical weapons pose a serious threat to the United States. After reading both viewpoints, explain which author's opinion you agree with, and why. Cite evidence from the text to bolster your answer.

The United States Should Pursue Diplomacy with Rogue Nations That Seek WMD

Susan E. Rice

Susan E. Rice is a Senior Fellow in Foreign Policy Studies at the Brookings Institution, from which this viewpoint was taken. In the following viewpoint, Rice discusses North Korea's acquisition of nuclear weapons. She argues that in order to prevent North Korea from using its new technology, or selling it to a terrorist group, the U.S. must engage the North Korean regime in a series of high-level talks. Although the Bush Administration has eschewed direct negotiations with North Korea in order to punish its leader, Kim Jong Il, Rice argues that those rules no longer apply now that Il has the power to use nuclear weapons in an attack. She urges the administration to swallow its pride and to engage the rogue regime in diplomatic talks in order to get it to give up its nuclear weapons.

Consider the Following Questions:

1. What three options does America have for dealing with North Korea, in Rice's opinion?
2. What does the term "arms race" mean in the context of the viewpoint?
3. Why does Rice think there is nothing to lose by engaging North Korean leader Kim Jong Il in bilateral talks?

"That horse is out of the barn," said actor and former Republican senator Fred Thompson when asked about North Korea's nuclear program. Thompson spoke at the premiere of "Last Best Chance," a chillingly realistic film sponsored by the Nuclear Threat Initiative. In it, he plays a president who fails to prevent al Qaeda from smuggling stolen nukes into the United States, dramatizing the imperative to halt proliferation at its source.

An Urgent Crisis

President Bush agrees that the greatest threat we face is nuclear weapons in the hands of terrorists. If, indeed, the North Korean horse "is out of the barn," we face a grave risk. To date, President Bush has failed to prevent North Korea from producing enough fissile material to build an estimated six to eight nuclear weapons, up from one to two in 2003.

Though administration officials have played down the significance of North Korea's growing arsenal, the threat to the United States has greatly increased. Impoverished North Korea now probably has enough nuclear material to sell its surplus to the highest bidder and still retain its own stockpile. Al Qaeda, which aims to use weapons of mass destruction against the United States, could be that bidder.

> ## Let's Talk to North Korea
>
> "It may be righteous, denying North Korea the reward of bilateral talks, but it has failed to secure U.S. interests."
>
> Robert L. Galluci, "Let's Make a Deal..." *Time*, October 23, 2006, p. 38.

We face an urgent crisis. In recent weeks North Korea has declared that it has nuclear weapons, has prepared to harvest plutonium sufficient for two more bombs and has hinted that it might conduct a nuclear test. If North Korea tests a nuclear weapon, there is little hope of reversing its nuclear program or of averting a regional arms race.

At this late stage, the United States has three options.

Three Options for America

First, we could strike North Korea's suspected nuclear facilities or use force to change the regime. Military options must remain on the table, but all of them are problematic. U.S. intelligence on North Korea is poor. Overstretched in Iraq, the United States does not have ground forces for an invasion. South Korea and China vehemently oppose military action. Worse still, North Korea could retaliate with a nuclear or conventional strike on nearby Seoul, on our more than 30,000 U.S. troops in South Korea, on Japan or even on the United States.

Second, we could accept a nuclear North Korea. But its erratic leader, Kim Jong Il, could still try to sell excess fissile material. He may also have the ability to attach a nuclear warhead to a long-range missile and hit the continental United States. Unfortunately, containment depends on two unreliable tools: national missile defense, which tests have proved is still hit-or-miss, and the proliferation security initiative—a seaborne, needle-in-the-haystack search complicated further by the refusal of China and South Korea to participate.

Third, the United States could pursue intensive bilateral negotiations within the framework of the Chinese-led six-party talks. Having dubbed North Korea and Iran charter members of the "axis of evil," the administration trades insults with those regimes while rejecting direct negotiations with "tyrants" and cheaters as repugnant. They are indeed, but not nearly as repugnant as a nuclear attack by terrorists on an American city.

Spent nuclear fuel rods from North Korea's Yongbyon nuclear reactor, in storage in a cooling pond.

Talking to North Korea

Together, six nations – the U.S., Russia, Japan, North Korea, South Korea, and China – have embarked on a series of diplomatic discussions called the Six-Party Talks to help disarm North Korea of its nuclear weapons. North Korea became the world's ninth nuclear power in 2006.

Russia

North Korea

USA

China

Japan

South Korea

We Need to Talk to North Korea Immediately

The president should recognize that rolling back North Korea's nuclear program is more important to U.S. national security than any principled objection to direct negotiations or tacit ambitions to change that odious regime. He should immediately propose high-level, bilateral talks and personally confirm that the United States has "no hostile intent" toward North Korea. In exchange for the "complete, verifiable and irreversible" dismantling of North Korea's nuclear programs, the United States should offer security guarantees, economic ties, fuel supplies and diplomatic relations.

제8차 북남상급회담
주체 91(2002)년 10월 19일-22일 평양

At this eleventh hour, North Korea might refuse the bilateral talks it has long sought, or such negotiations could well fail. Yet a serious effort to negotiate is critical to any hope of gaining eventual South Korean or Chinese assent to punitive action. If direct negotiations fail, President Bush will merely face the same choice he does today: launch a potentially catastrophic war on the Korean Peninsula or allow North Korea to expand its nuclear arsenal, hoping we can catch any bombs it might sell before they cross our borders.

South Korean (left) and North Korean diplomats discuss North Korea's weapons program at a 2002 conference. Disarming North Korea is a priority for South Korea, its closest neighbor.

Talks Are Our Last Best Chance

There is speculation that the administration may decide to seek U.N. sanctions against North Korea and, if China vetoes them or refuses to exert major pressure, blame China for this crisis. Primary responsibility rests with North Korea, but for too long the administration has relegated the problem to the sidelines and subcontracted U.S. policy to China, whose interests differ substantially from ours. To now blame China or seek unattainable sanctions would be posturing, not responsible policy.

Time is not on our side. The president needs to act swiftly to eliminate North Korea's nuclear program—through intense bilateral diplomacy. A continued refusal to try would squander our "last best chance" to salvage a nightmarish policy failure.

Analyze the Essay:

1. Rice believes America's best chance of avoiding disaster is to engage North Korea in direct, bilateral talks. Anatol Lieven and John Hulsman, authors of the following viewpoint, believe that countries more immediately threatened by North Korea should be responsible for engaging it in talks. What do you think—is it America's responsibility to pursue diplomacy with North Korea or not? Explain your opinion.

2. Rice suggests that the United States should offer North Korea certain rewards in exchange for dismantling its nuclear weapons program. What are these rewards? In your opinion, is this a good tactic for getting North Korea to abandon its weapons program? Why or why not?

The United States Should Not Pursue Diplomacy with Rogue Nations That Seek WMD

Anatol Lieven and John Hulsman

In the following viewpoint, authors Anatol Lieven and John Hulsman argue that although North Korea is not to be trusted with nuclear weapons, it is not America's job to get involved with fixing the problem. The authors argue that America is already overcommitted militarily: it has troops on multiple continents and is barely able to keep up with military challenges around the world. North Korea poses a greater threat to its neighbors than to the United States, the authors argue—if North Korea were to launch a nuclear attack, its neighbors would be in the front lines of danger, not the United States. Therefore, the authors conclude that the United States should let China, South Korea, Japan, and Russia handle the effort and costs of confronting North Korea—the United States has its own problems to deal with.

Anatol Lieven is a senior research fellow at the New America Foundation in Washington, D.C. John Hulsman is a scholar in residence at the German Council on Foreign Relations in Berlin. Their new book is *Ethical Realism: A Vision for America's Role in the World*.

Anatol Lieven and John Hulsman, "North Korea's Not Our Problem," *Los Angeles Times*, October 11, 2006, p. B13. Copyright © 2006 Los Angeles Times. Reproduced by permission of the authors.

Consider the Following Questions:
1. Name four global conflicts the United States is currently involved in, as reported by the authors.
2. What does the word "isolationism" mean in the context of the viewpoint?
3. How many U.S. troops are stationed on the Korean Peninsula, as reported by the authors?

The United States is bogged down in what appears to be an unwinnable war in Iraq; it is facing very unpleasant options in regard to neighboring Iran's nuclear program; senior NATO officers say that the situation in Afghanistan is deteriorating fast; in the former Soviet Union, Georgia and Russia are moving toward military confrontation, with the U.S. seemingly unable to restrain either; in large swaths of Latin America, new nationalist and populist movements are challenging U.S. interests.

And now the totalitarian regime in North Korea has defied the international community by testing a nuclear bomb—and the U.S. appears to have neither military nor effective economic measures with which to respond.

The U.S. Is Overextended

If all this does not prove the reality of American overreach, what does? If U.S. power is to be placed on a firmer basis, its exercise must be more limited. Certain commitments will have to be scaled back or even eliminated if the U.S. is to be able to concentrate on dealing with its most truly vital challenges and enemies.

This is not an argument for isolationism but for the kind of calm, clearheaded global strategy adopted in the past by American leaders such as Franklin D. Roosevelt, Dwight

Assistant Secretary of State Christopher Hill, the lead American diplomat assigned to the North Korean nuclear issue, after a meeting with South Korean diplomats in 2007.

Eisenhower and Richard Nixon: a morally courageous willingness to recognize the greatest threats to the U.S. and to deal with secondary concerns accordingly. When Roosevelt formed an alliance with the Soviet Union against Hitler, or Nixon went to China to do a deal with Chairman Mao, it was assuredly not because they admired the Stalinist or Maoist systems or were prepared to sacrifice vital U.S. interests to them.

Charles de Gaulle defined the nature of statesmanship when he said that "to govern is to choose—usually between unpleasant alternatives." This is something that the U.S. is finding it increasingly difficult to do. For it is torn among a multitude of different domestic lobbies and presided over by an administration that has grossly overestimated U.S. power.

North Korea Is Not America's Problem

In consequence, it has involved itself in fights in several different parts of the world simultaneously, sometimes over trivial issues.

Consider, for example, that at a time when the U.S. is facing crises of truly vital importance in the Middle East, it is also drifting toward a dangerous confrontation with Russia, a key player in the Middle East, over … South Ossetia.

What next, we wonder? Massive U.S. involvement in a Chilean-Argentine conflict over control of the Beagle Channel? A huge commitment of U.S. energy and resources to help Paraguay recover the Gran Chaco?

There is one region that the U.S. can and should bow out of now: Korea. North Korea's bomb test is obviously a very serious problem for the U.S., given its heavy military presence in South Korea. However, we should ask why, more than 50 years after the Korean War and 15 years after the end of the Cold War, the United States still has about 37,500 troops on the Korean peninsula.

Less Talk, More Action

"Doves profess concern about Iran's nuclear program and endorse various diplomatic responses to it. But they don't want even to contemplate the threat of military action. Perhaps military action won't ultimately be necessary. But the only way diplomatic, political, and economic pressure has a chance to work over the next months is if the military option—or various military options—are kept on the table."

William Kristol, "And Now Iran; We Can't Rule Out the Use of Military Force," *Weekly Standard*, January 23, 2006.

North Korea's Neighbors Should Pursue Diplomacy—Not the U.S.

In the long run, North Korea's nuclear weapons are an overwhelming problem only for its neighbors, and it should be their responsibility to sort this problem out. Of course, they may fail—but then, the U.S. record in the region over the last decade has not exactly been one of success.

The U.S. is already reducing its troop levels on the Korean peninsula; it should accelerate the process and move rapidly toward ending its military presence. Moreover, it should negotiate a peace treaty with North Korea. This will remove Pyongyang's motive to attack U.S. interests, ensure that China could never again attack U.S. forces in a ground war and allow the U.S. to concentrate instead on maintaining its overwhelming lead over China in naval and air power.

South Korean envoy Chun Yung-woo (left) shakes hands with his North Korean counterpart Kim Kye Gwan during a July 18, 2007, meeting in Beijing, China. The United Nations had just confirmed that North Korea had shut down its main nuclear complex, seen as an important step in dealing with the North Korean nuclear issue.

We must be very clear, however, that this withdrawal would also mean ceding to China the dominant role in containing North Korea's nuclear ambitions—along with Japan, South Korea and Russia—and in managing the eventual collapse of the North Korean state and the appallingly difficult and expensive process of the reunification of the two Koreas.

Sympathetic But Distant

Given how costly and difficult reunification has proved to be for the Germanys after the fall of the Berlin Wall, we should be only too happy to throw this particular time bomb into China's lap. It would grant Beijing international prestige and an extra share of regional influence in an area vital to its interests, while saving us great costs and dangers.

North Korea must be treated as a regional problem to be managed by a regional concert of powers, with China in the lead. The U.S. role in all this should be sympathetic—and distant.

Analyze the Essay:

1. To make their argument, the authors use historical figures and situations. After examining which historical figures and situations they mention, choose one example to focus on. Explain what comparisons the authors are making and what bearing history has on the present problem with North Korea.

2. The authors conclude that the U.S. should bow out of the North Korea problem based on the fact that the United States military is already occupied elsewhere in the world. How do you think Susan E. Rice, author of the previous viewpoint, would react to this suggestion?

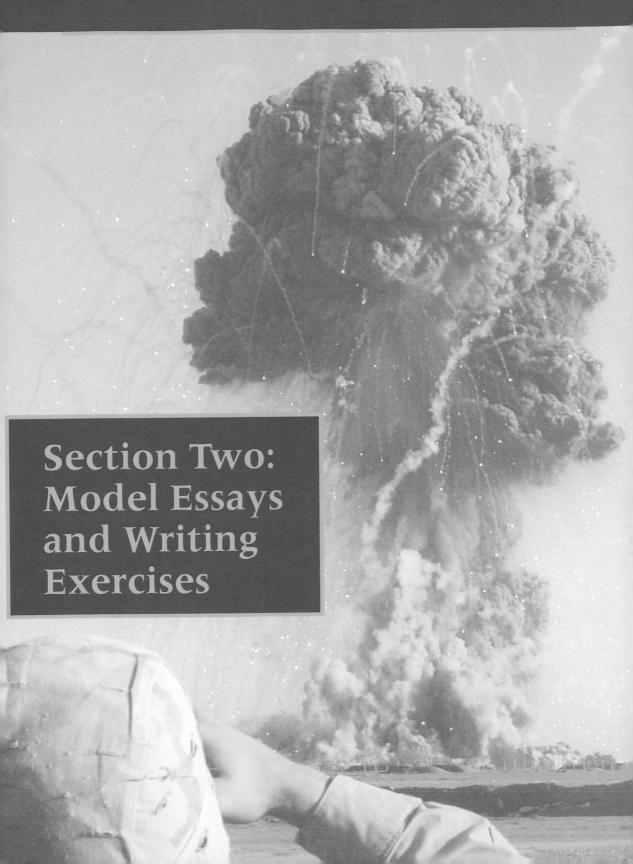

Section Two:
Model Essays
and Writing
Exercises

The Five-Paragraph Essay

An *essay* is a short piece of writing that discusses or analyzes one topic. The five-paragraph essay is a form commonly used in school assignments and tests. Every five-paragraph essay begins with an *introduction*, ends with a *conclusion*, and features three *supporting paragraphs* in the middle.

The Thesis Statement. The introduction includes the essay's thesis statement. The thesis statement presents the argument or point the author is trying to make about the topic. The essays in this book all have different thesis statements because they are making different arguments about weapons of mass destruction.

The thesis statement should clearly tell the reader what the essay will be about. A focused thesis statement helps determine what will be in the essay; the subsequent paragraphs are spent developing and supporting its argument.

The Introduction. In addition to presenting the thesis statement, a well-written introductory paragraph captures the attention of the reader and explains why the topic being explored is important. It may provide the reader with background information on the subject matter or feature an anecdote that illustrates a point relevant to the topic. It could also present startling information that clarifies the point of the essay or put forth a contradictory position that the essay will refute. Further techniques for writing an introduction are found later in this section.

The Supporting Paragraphs. The introduction is then followed by three (or more) supporting paragraphs. These are the main body of the essay. Each paragraph presents and develops a *subtopic* that supports the essay's thesis statement. Each *subtopic* is spearheaded by a *topic sentence* and supported by its own facts, details, and examples. The writer can use various kinds of supporting material and details to back up the topic of each supporting paragraph. These may include statistics, quotations from people with special knowledge or expertise, historic facts, and anecdotes. A rule of writing is that specific and concrete examples are more convincing than vague, general, or unsupported assertions.

The Conclusion. The conclusion is the paragraph that closes the essay. Its function is to summarize or reiterate the main idea of the essay. It may recall an idea from the introduction or briefly examine the larger implications of the thesis. Because the conclusion is also the last chance a writer has to make an impression on the reader, it is important that it not simply repeat what has been presented elsewhere in the essay but close it in a clear, final, and memorable way.

Although the order of the essay's component paragraphs is important, they do not have to be written in the order presented here. Some writers like to decide on a thesis and write the introduction paragraph first. Other writers like to focus first on the body of the essay, and write the introduction and conclusion later.

Pitfalls to Avoid

When writing essays about controversial issues such as weapons of mass destruction, it is important to remember that disputes over the material are common precisely because there are many different perspectives. Remember to state your arguments in careful and measured terms. Evaluate your topic fairly—avoid overstating negative qualities of one perspective or understating positive qualities of another. Use examples, facts, and details to support any assertions you make.

The Expository Essay

The previous section of this book provided you with samples of writings on weapons of mass destruction. All made arguments or advocated a particular position about weapons of mass destruction and related topics. All included elements of *expository* writing as well. The purpose of expository writing is to inform the reader about a particular subject matter. Sometimes a writer will use exposition to simply communicate knowledge; at other times, he or she will use exposition to persuade a reader of a particular point of view.

Types of Expository Writing

There are several different types of expository writing. Examples of these types can be found in the viewpoints in the preceding chapter. The list below provides some ideas on how exposition could be organized and presented. Each type of writing could be used separately or in combination in five-paragraph essays.

- *Definition*. Definition refers to simply telling what something is. Definitions can be encompassed in a sentence or paragraph. At other times, definitions may take a paragraph or more. The act of defining some topics—especially abstract concepts—can sometimes serve as the focus of entire essays. An example of definition is found in Viewpoint 3 by Bill Frist. He spends a large portion of his essay defining what biological weapons are, how they work, and explaining their effects.
- *Classification*. A classification essay describes and clarifies relationships between things by placing them in different categories, based on their similarities and differences. This can be a good way of organizing and presenting information.

- *Process.* A process essay looks at how something is done. The writer presents events or steps in a chronological or ordered sequence of steps. Process writing can either inform the reader of a past event or process by which something was made, or instruct the reader on how to do something. William Perry uses process in Viewpoint 1 when he outlines steps that can be taken to curb the spread of nuclear weapons.
- *Illustration.* Illustration is one of the simplest and most common patterns of expository writing. Simply put, it explains by giving specific and concrete examples. It is an effective technique for making one's writing both more interesting and more intelligible.
- *Problem/Solution.* Problem/Solution refers to when the author raises a problem or a question, then uses the rest of the paragraph or essay to answer the question or provide possible resolutions to the problem. It can be an effective way of drawing in the reader while imparting information to him/her. The author of Viewpoint 5, Susan E. Rice, uses problem/solution to argue that the U.S. should pursue diplomatic relations with North Korea. She raises the problem of North Korea's possession of nuclear weapons and proposes solving that problem by using diplomacy to disarm North Korea. Likewise, the authors of Viewpoint 6 use problem/solution. They raise the same problem as Rice, but suggest solving it by letting North Korea's neighbors deal with the threat posed by the nation.

Words and Phrases Common to Expository Essays

accordingly

because

consequently

clearly

first…second…third…

for example

for this reason

from this perspective

furthermore

evidently

however

indeed

it is important to understand

it makes sense to

it seems as though

it then follows that

moreover

since

subsequently

therefore

this is why

thus

How Nuclear Weapons Were Invented

Editor's Notes The first model essay is a "process" expository essay that explains how nuclear weapons were invented. As explained in Preface B on expository techniques, process essays present information in a chronological or ordered sequence of steps. Process writing can either instruct the reader on how to do something or inform the reader of a past event. The following essay tells readers how nuclear weapons were invented.

Note that the following essay is a classic expository essay because it does not promote a particular point of view or argument. Each paragraph contains supporting details and information, much of which was taken from resources found in Section I and Section III of this book. As you read the essay, pay attention to its components and how it is organized. Also note that all sources are cited using Modern Language Association (MLA) style.* For more information on how to cite your sources see Appendix C. In addition, consider the following:

■ Refers to thesis and topic sentences

■ Refers to supporting details

- How does the introduction engage the reader's attention?
- What pieces of supporting evidence are used to back up the essay's arguments?
- What purpose do the essay's quotes serve?
- How does the author transition from one idea to another?

*Editor's Note: In applying MLA style guidelines in this book, the following simplifications have been made: Parenthetical text citations are confined to direct quotations only; electronic source documentation in the Works Cited list omits date of access, page ranges, and some detailed facts of publication.

Paragraph 1

Some Americans are surprised to learn that only one nation has ever dropped nuclear bombs during any conflict: the United States. The United States was also first to posses the simultaneously awesome and awful nuclear weaponry. Indeed, nuclear weapons were developed by American scientists to help win World War II and to place the U.S. in a strategically strong position at the end of that war. Understanding the origins of nuclear weapons helps shed light on their importance and use today.

This is the essay's thesis statement. It lets the reader know what the essay will be about.

Paragraph 2

Nuclear weapons were invented by the U.S. Army Corps of Engineers during the early 1940s under a project called the Manhattan Project. Under the Manhattan Project, some of America's most famous scientists, including Albert Einstein and J. Robert Oppenheimer, worked to develop the most powerful weapon the world had ever seen. The scientists spent four years and $2 billion (which would amount to more than $23 billion in today's dollars) developing military applications of nuclear fission technology. Their efforts resulted in three weapons: a bomb code-named "Little Boy" that could deliver a 15 kiloton explosion (equal to exploding 15,000 tons of TNT); one code-named "Fat Man" that was rated at 20 kilotons, and a third 20 kiloton weapon that was intended for testing.

This is the topic sentence of Paragraph 2. It lets the reader know this paragraph will focus on the Manhattan Project. This is the first step to telling the story of how nuclear weapons were invented.

The highlighted details are all specific, and thus give substance to the essay. Always include specific rather than general pieces of information in your essays.

Paragraph 3

Before the weapon was used in combat, the military wanted to test it to learn about the damage it would cause. So on July 16, 1945, in a test called the Trinity Test, scientists chose a remote desert section of the Alamogordo Air Base 120 miles southeast of Albuquerque, New Mexico, to explode the test weapon. The explosion was more violent and powerful than anything anyone had ever witnessed. The explosion from the bomb left a crater that was 10 feet deep and 1100 feet wide, or the length of more than 3 football fields. The blast also

This is the topic sentence of Paragraph 3. It focuses on a new yet related topic.

produced a shockwave that was felt by observers more than 100 miles away, while a mushroom cloud from the explosion extended more than 7 miles into the atmosphere. The surrounding air became incredibly hot, and the explosion lit up the surrounding desert as if it were high noon. General Thomas F. Farrell, who witnessed the explosion, said, "The lighting effects beggared description. The whole country was lighted by a searing light with the intensity many times that of the midday sun. It was golden, purple, violet, gray, and blue. It lighted every peak, crevasse and ridge of the nearby mountain range with a clarity and beauty that cannot be described but must be seen to be imagined." (qtd in "War Department Release on New Mexico Test")

> Note the use of specific details to paint a picture of what the explosion was like.

> This quote provides a first-person perspective that you as an objective author could not provide. Quotes like this bring life to your essays.

Paragraph 4

Not long after the Trinity test, the U.S.'s new weapons were used in wartime. "Little Boy" was detonated over the Japanese city of Hiroshima on August 6, 1945. About 140,000 people were killed by the initial blast and its aftermath. Three days later, the U.S. military dropped its second bomb, "Fat Man," over the Japanese city of Nagasaki. It is estimated that approximately 70,000 people were killed in Nagasaki by the bomb's explosion and its aftermath. U.S. leaders had intended the bombs to be so devastating they would bring the Japanese to their knees, and that was exactly what happened. Japan surrendered to the U.S. and its allies days later, and the war ended shortly afterwards.

> What is the topic sentence of Paragraph 4? How did you recognize it?

> What supporting details are used in Paragraph 4?

Paragraph 5

The dropping of nuclear weapons on Japan may have ended World War II, but it began another war, one that would last for the next half a century: the Cold War. Indeed, immediately following the end of World War II, the Soviet Union made it a priority to counter the newfound influence of the U.S. by developing its own nuclear weapons. The Soviets began pursuing bomb research on their own and in 1949, after a

> Rather than summarizing what has been discussed, the final paragraph provides an aftermath of the story that has been presented.

combination of scientific research and espionage, successfully tested a nuclear weapon that was the same size and strength of the Fat Man bomb dropped on Nagasaki. The nuclear arms race had begun. The two superpowers began a weapons build-up the likes of which had never been seen. It is this very arsenal that world leaders today are actively trying to decommission and account for in the race to prevent terrorists from acquiring nuclear weapons.

The conclusion returns to the initial point raised in the essay's introduction: the impact that the development of nuclear weapons has on today's world.

Works Cited

"War Department Release on New Mexico Test," U.S. Army 16 Jul. 1945. http://www.atomicarchive.com/Docs/Trinity/PressRelease.shtml Accessed June 19, 2007.

Exercise 1A: Create an Outline from an Existing Essay

It often helps to create an outline of the five-paragraph essay before you write it. The outline can help you organize the information, arguments, and evidence you have gathered during your research.

For this exercise, create an outline that could have been used to write *How Nuclear Weapons Were Invented*. Identify topic sentences and provide at least two supporting details for each sentence. This "reverse engineering" exercise is meant to help familiarize you with how outlines can help classify and arrange information.

To do this you will need to;
1. articulate the essay's thesis;
2. pinpoint important pieces of evidence;
3. flag quotes that supported the essay's ideas; and
4. identify key points that supported the argument.

Part of the outline has already been started to give you an idea of the assignment.

Outline

I. **Paragraph One**

   A. Write the essay's thesis: Nuclear weapons were developed by American scientists to help win World War II and to place the U.S. in a strategically strong position at the end of that war.

II. **Paragraph Two**

   Topic:

A. Alfred Einstein and J. Robert Oppenheimer worked on the Manhattan Project

B. Three weapons were produced by the Manhattan Project: "Little Boy," "Fat Man," and a third 20 kiloton weapon that was intended for testing.

III. Paragraph Three

Topic:

A. The explosion from the bomb left a crater that was 10 feet deep and 1100 feet wide, or the length of more than 3 football fields.

B. Quote from General Farrell explaining what the blast looked like.

IV. Paragraph Four

Topic:

A.

B.

V. Paragraph Five

A. Write the essay's conclusion:

Terrorists Are Not Likely to Acquire Biochemical Weapons

Editor's Notes One way of writing an expository essay is to use the illustration method. When expository essays use illustration, they explain their point using specific and concrete examples. Illustration is an effective technique for making one's writing both more interesting and more intelligible. The following sample essay uses illustration techniques to argue that terrorists are not likely to acquire and use biochemical weapons in a terrorist attack. The author uses clear and concrete examples to support her argument.

This essay differs from the first model essay in that it is also a persuasive essay, meaning that the author wants to persuade you to agree with her point of view. As you read, keep track of the notes in the margins. They will help you analyze how the essay is organized and how it is written.

■ Refers to thesis and topic sentences

■ Refers to supporting details

Paragraph 2

A growing concern since the terrorist attacks of September 11th is whether terrorists would launch a terrorist attack using biological or chemical agents. Certainly, if such an attack occurred, it could be devastating. According to an Office of Technology Assessment report prepared for the federal government, 1000 kilograms of sarin gas, a chemical weapon, dispersed over a large American city could kill 300–8,000 people, while an attack using a biological agent such as anthrax could kill between 130,000 and 3 million. But before people start to panic, it is worth asking: are terrorists actually likely to pull off such an attack? Both history and the nature of biological and chemical agents say such an attack is not likely.

This point somewhat undermines the point of this essay. Why do you think the author chose to open the essay with it?

What is the essay's thesis statement? How did you recognize it?

This is the topic sentence of Paragraph 2. It is focused on one idea that supports the essay's thesis.

Many experts argue that while a biochemical attack is very frightening, in truth, it would be hard to properly pull off. Because such agents are unstable and very sensitive, they are difficult to be successfully manufactured for use in an attack (a process called weaponization). For example, a biological or chemical agent might be difficult to weaponize if it was an impure strain, or mishandled and exposed to elements that would render it ineffective (some agents are rendered harmless once exposed to cooler or warmer temperatures, for example). Furthermore, climactic conditions such as wind, rain, cloud cover and temperature, as well as the quality of the dispersal method, can all interfere with a biochemical attack's potency and success. For this reason Milton Leitenberg, a bioweapons scholar, says, "Bioterrorism may or may not develop into a serious concern in the future, but it is *not* one of the most pressing problems that we have on the planet today." (87)

This quote was taken from the quote box accompanying Viewpoint 4. This book contains many quotes that can be used to support points in your essays.

Paragraph 3

In what way are expository techniques worked into the essay? List at least 3 examples.

Given their difficulty to weaponize, it is not surprising that biochemical attacks are exceedingly rare. In fact, there have only been 3 biochemical terrorist attacks in recent history. Furthermore, none of these has been very successful. One attack occurred in 1984, when a cult called Rajneeshee poisoned salad bars in Oregon. Seven hundred and fifty one people were sickened, but no one was killed. Another attack was perpetrated in 1995 by the Japanese terrorist group Aum Shinrikyo. The Japanese terrorists released sarin gas on Tokyo subway system, killing 12 people and harming more than 50. Finally, in 2001, an anonymous terrorist or terrorist group sent anthrax-laced letters through the U.S. Postal Service, infecting 17 and killing five. Though each of these attacks frightened thousands, only 17 lives have been taken by this type of terrorism. This is hardly enough to constitute one of the gravest and greatest threats facing Americans today.

The author is expressing her opinion in this sentence. Note how it interprets the factual information that preceded it.

Paragraph 4

Because of the minimal threat posed by biochemical weapons, many scientists disapprove of the large amounts of federal funding that have gone into thwarting such an attack. Indeed, millions have been spent on such programs—in 2004, for example, President George W. Bush approved Project BioShield, which allocates more than $1 billion to develop antidotes, vaccines, and treatment in the event of a biochemical attack. Because the threat of such attacks is low, many scientists argue these precious dollars are being directed away from more important medical research on diseases and problems that kill far more people. As molecular biologist Richard Ebright says, "Bioweapons agents cause, on average, zero deaths per year in the United States, in contrast to a broad range of [other] pathogens that cause tens or hundreds of thousands of deaths per year." (1409–1410)

What is the topic sentence of Paragraph 4? How does it relate to the essay's thesis statement?

What transitional words and phrases are used in this essay? Make a list of all that appear.

Paragraph 5

Therefore, while a terrorist attack using biological or chemical weapons is certainly a frightening idea, it is not likely to become a reality for years to come, if ever. For this reason, politicians should rethink spending so much on biochemical weapon defense when the money is surely needed in other areas. America should not make its policy and funding decisions based on fear, but sound science. Otherwise, as journalist Allison MacFarlane has warned, we will end up "spending billions of dollars defending ourselves against ghosts, and in the process putting these weapons on a pedestal."

Note how the conclusion does not merely summarize what has been stated in the essay, but makes suggestions for how to move forward.

Works Cited

"Letter". *Science* Vol. 307. no. 5714 4 Mar. 2005: 1409–1410.

Leitenberg, Milton. "Assessing the Biological Weapons and Bioterrorism Threat." *Strategic Studies Institute* Dec. 2005: 87.

Macfarlane, Allison. "All Weapons of Mass Destruction Are Not Equal," Alternet.com. 8 Feb. 2006. <www.alternet.org/story/31510> Accessed June 17, 2007.

Exercise 2A: Create an Outline from an Existing Essay

As you did for the first model essay in this section, create an outline that could have been used to write *Terrorists Are Not Likely to Acquire Biochemical Weapons*. Be sure to identify the essay's thesis statement, its supporting ideas, its descriptive passages, and key pieces of evidence that were used.

Exercise 2B: Create an Outline for Your Own Essay

The second model essay expresses a particular point of view about weapons of mass destruction. For this exercise, your assignment is to find supporting ideas, choose specific and concrete details, create an outline, and ultimately write a five-paragraph essay making a different, or even opposing, point about weapons of mass destruction. Your goal is to use expository and persuasive techniques to convince your reader.

Step I: Write a Thesis Statement
The following thesis statement would be appropriate for an opposing essay on why the government must put resources towards defending against a biochemical terrorist attack:

> We cannot predict whether terrorists will attempt an attack using biochemical warfare, but we must be prepared for the possibility: the devastation that could be wreaked by an attack involving pathogens such as small-pox, anthrax, or the plague could quickly spread around the globe, victimizing the entire human race.

Or see the sample paper topics suggested in Appendix D for more ideas.

Step II: Brainstorm Pieces of Supporting Evidence

Using information from some of the viewpoints in the previous section and from the information found in Section III of this book, write down three arguments or pieces of evidence that support the thesis statement you selected. Then, for each of these three arguments, write down supportive facts, examples, and details that support it. These could be:

- statistical information.
- personal memories and anecdotes.
- quotes from experts, peers, or family members.
- observations of people's actions and behaviors.
- specific and concrete details.

Supporting pieces of evidence for the above sample thesis statement are found in this book, and include:

- Quote from Leonard A. Cole in the box in Viewpoint 3 about how bioweapons are relatively easy to manufacture, and someone with biological knowledge and materials could do so in a matter of weeks.
- Quote by former Senator Bill Frist in Viewpoint 3 about how devastating a biochemical attack would be: "The greatest existential threat we have in the world today is biological. Why? Because unlike any other threat it has the power of panic and paralysis to be global."
- Information in Appendix A about the deadly effects of various biological and chemical weapons.

Step III: Place the information from Step I in outline form.

Step IV: Write the arguments or supporting statements in paragraph form.

By now you have three arguments that support the essay's thesis statement, as well as supporting material. Use the outline to write out your three supporting arguments in paragraph form. Make sure each paragraph has a topic sentence that states the paragraph's thesis clearly and broadly. Then, add supporting sentences that express the facts, quotes, details, and examples that support the paragraph's argument. The paragraph may also have a concluding or summary sentence.

The Devastating Power of Nuclear Weapons

Editor's Notes Yet another way of writing an expository essay is to use the definition method. A definition expository essay generally tells what something is. Definitions can be encompassed in a sentence or paragraph. At other times, definitions may take a paragraph or more, and even be the focus of entire essays. Such is the case in the final model essay. The writer defines what nuclear weapons are and what they are capable of.

This essay differs from the previous model essays in that it is longer than five paragraphs. Sometimes five paragraphs are simply not enough to adequately develop an idea. Extending the length of an essay can allow the reader to explore a topic in more depth or present multiple pieces of evidence that together provide a complete picture of a topic. Longer essays can also help readers discover the complexity of a subject by examining a topic beyond its superficial exterior. Moreover, the ability to write a sustained research or position paper is a valuable skill you will need as you advance academically.

As you read, consider the questions posed in the margins. Continue to identify thesis statements, supporting details, transitions, and quotations. Examine the introductory and concluding paragraphs to understand how they give shape to the essay. Finally, evaluate the essay's general structure and assess its overall effectiveness.

Refers to thesis and topic sentences

Refers to supporting details

The essay begins with an anecdote related to the essay's theme. See Exercise 3B at the end of this essay for more information on writing interesting and engaging introductions.

Paragraph 1

When American physicist J. Robert Oppenheimer witnessed the first atomic bomb test on July 16, 1945, a single phrase from the sacred Hindu text, the Bhagavad-Gita, ran through his mind: "Now I am become Death, the destroyer of worlds." Oppenheimer's thoughts stemmed from the utter destruction he realized the weapon he had helped build could unleash on humanity. Indeed, the politics surrounding nuclear weapons are often hotly debated, but rarely does anyone describe what a nuclear explosion would actually be like. Examining the devastating power of the world's most powerful weapon, however, is enough to give anyone pause. The horrific details that follow should be kept in mind when people discuss the political and economic implications of weapons of mass destruction.

What is the essay's thesis statement? How is it different from the thesis statements of the other model essays in this section?

Paragraph 2

The explosion from a nuclear weapon—even a small one, such as the 15 or 20 kiloton bombs dropped on the Japanese cities of Hiroshima and Nagasaki that ended World War II—would cause an explosion of unimaginable power. The blast would consist of a chemical reaction that would release a tremendous amount of energy—about 300 trillion calories in a fraction of a second. Put another way, this energy would form a light brighter than 5,000 suns, and then trigger an enormous fireball that would be about 200 million degrees hot, or more than 4 times the temperature at the sun's center!

Make a list of all transitional words and phrases used in the essay. Pay attention to how they keep the ideas in the essay moving.

Paragraph 3

The fireball would build, collecting energy by burning everything in its path. Quickly the fireball would transform itself into a firestorm, a powerful swirl of heat and wind that would incinerate everything in the surrounding area. Indeed, most of the destruction wrought by a nuclear weapon would stem not from the initial blast, but from this firestorm. Author Russell D. Hoffman asks readers to picture the apocalyptic scene in the following way: "The fire burns so hot that the asphalt in the streets begins to melt and then burn, even as people are trying to run across it, literally melting into the pavement themselves as they run. Victims, on fire, jump into rivers, only to catch fire again when they surface for air."

What is the topic sentence of Paragraph 3? What details are used to support it?

Note how the Hoffman quote paints a detailed picture—does it enhance your ability to visualize the devastation?

Paragraph 4

It is almost impossible to comprehend how hot the area within the firestorm would be. Scientists who have modeled the effects of a nuclear explosion using computers predict that average air temperatures would be well above boiling. Most life would be instantly incinerated. Furthermore, if lakes, rivers or ponds were in the area of the firestorm, their contents would immediately begin to boil and bubble. Even those who managed to get to bomb shelters might not survive because the temperatures inside of them would be too hot to sustain life.

What kinds of details are included to help bring the essay to life?

Paragraph 5

What is the topic sentence of Paragraph 5? How does it fit within the essay's thesis?

In addition to wreaking havoc on the blast site, the nuclear explosion would release large amounts of deadly radiation into the air. Radiation is a type of energy that can be tolerated by humans in small doses (such as the small amount in x-rays). But in large doses, exposure to radiation can be very dangerous. Indeed if a nuclear bomb were to be exploded over a modern urban area, it would cause radiation sickness, cancer, and death in thousands, even millions, of people. Explains one team of scientists: "Radiation exposure could lead to a variety of symptoms such as nausea, bloody diarrhea, and hemorrhages within a few days (other consequences of radiation could appear years later). These health effects are often fatal and include leukemia, thyroid cancer, breast cancer, and lung cancer, as well as non-fatal diseases such as birth defects, cataracts, [and] mental retardation in young children." (McKinzie, Mian, Ramana, Nayyar, 3)

What kinds of experts are quoted in the essay? Make a list of their qualifications.

Paragraph 6

Radiation would cause the slow and painful death of thousands of people in the blast area. In effect, the radiation would cause body cells to begin breaking down at the molecular level. Hoffman describes the effect this would have on the body's organs in a particularly visceral way,

"The insides of those who get a severe dose of gamma radiation, but manage to survive the other traumas, whose organs had once been well defined as lungs, liver, heart, intestines, etc., [would] begin to resemble an undefined mass of bloody pulp."

Paragraph 7

Even if some survived the initial effects of radiation, many others would inherit health problems that could last their entire lives. For example, thousands of survivors from Hiroshima and Nagasaki experienced increased rates of cancer, disease, and other health effects. Their children suffered higher than normal rates of stillborn death, mental retardation and other birth defects. Also, exposure to high levels of radiation has been proven to cause genetic mutations in laboratory animals, so some scientists believe those affected by radiation in Japan may carry genetic mutations that will reveal themselves in coming generations.

> What is the topic sentence of Paragraph 7? Does it focus on something that hasn't yet been touched upon in the essay?

Paragraph 8

It is impossible to know how many people would die in a nuclear bomb attack, but it is safe to say the number would be anywhere from tens of thousands to millions, depending on the size of the bomb. According to a 2006 study by University of Georgia scientists that simulated nuclear explosions over four American cities, a 20 kiloton bomb detonated in Chicago would kill about 614,000 people; a 550 kiloton bomb would kill about 3.4 million. Scientists estimate that a bomb of this size would decimate an area of between 12 and 65 square miles, depending on factors such as weather that would help or hinder the spread of the firestorm. All of this damage could be caused by just one bomb, let alone the dozens or even hundreds that could be launched in an all-out nuclear war. For this reason, scientists say "As remote as the possibility is, all-out nuclear war has the potential to end human life on the planet—still the true doomsday scenario." (Rothstein, Auer, and Siegel, 47)

> What facts or statistics have been used to support points made in the essay? From what kinds of sources has the author taken them from?

> What does this quote lend to Paragraph 8?

Paragraph 9

Indeed, the effects of nuclear war would be at once horrific and disastrous. "Anything that you can do to discourage people from thinking that there is any way to win anything with a nuclear exchange is a good idea," says scientist Stephen Schneider. "You [would] have to be mega-insane to think there is any political objective for which a nuclear explosion is going to do you any good." (qtd in Lee) The next time you read arguments about whether North Korea should be engaged in talks to disarm it of nuclear weapons, or whether the U.S. should use nuclear weapons in a war against terrorists, consider the on-the-ground realities of what a nuclear explosion would entail before you decide where you stand on the issue of weapons of mass destruction.

> Note how the conclusion returns to the idea introduced in the beginning of the essay. Learn how to bookend your essay with like ideas that do not summarize what has already been covered.

Works Cited

Hoffman, Russell D. "The Effects of a Nuclear War." Information Clearing House, 8 Aug. 2003. http://www.informationclearinghouse.info/article4394.htm Accessed June 17, 2007.

Lee, Brian D. "Climate scientist Stephen Schneider describes chilling consequences of a nuclear war." *Stanford Report* 10 Jan. 2007.

McKinzie, Matthew, Zia Mian, M.V. Ramana, and A.H. Nayyar. "Nuclear War in South Asia." *Foreign Policy in Focus* June 2002: 1-6. http://www.fpif.org/papers/nuclearsasia.html

Rothstein, Linda, Catherine Auer, and Jonas Siegel. "Rethinking Doomsday." *Bulletin of the Atomic Scientists* Nov.–Dec. 2004: 47.

Exercise 3A: Using Quotations to Enliven Your Essay

No essay is complete without quotations. Get in the habit of using quotes to support at least some of the ideas in your essays. Quotes do not need to appear in every paragraph, but often enough so that the essay contains voices aside from your own. When you write, use quotations to accomplish the following:

- Provide expert advice that you are not necessarily in the position to know about.
- Cite lively or passionate passages.
- Include a particularly well-written point that gets to the heart of the matter.
- Supply statistics or facts that have been derived from someone's research.
- Deliver anecdotes that illustrate the point you are trying to make.
- Express first-person testimony.

Problem One: Reread the essays presented in all sections of this book and find at least one example of each of the above quotation types.) come at the end of the page—and give it some space after the bulleted list.

There are a couple of important things to remember when using quotations.

- Note your sources' qualifications and biases. This way your reader can identify the person you have quoted and can put their words in a context.

Put any quoted material within proper quotation marks. Failing to attribute quotes to their authors constitutes plagiarism, which is when an author takes someone else's words or ideas and presents them as their own. Plagiarism is a form of intellectual theft and must be avoided at all costs.

Exercise 3B: Examining Introductions and Conclusions

Every essay features introductory and concluding paragraphs that are used to frame the main ideas being presented. Along with presenting the essay's thesis statement, well-written introductions should grab the attention of the reader and make clear why the topic being explored is important. The conclusion reiterates the essay's thesis and is also the last chance for the writer to make an impression on the reader. Strong introductions and conclusions can greatly enhance an essay's effect on an audience.

The Introduction

There are several techniques that can be used to craft an introductory paragraph. An essay can start with:

- an anecdote: a brief story that illustrates a point relevant to the topic.
- startling information: facts or statistics that elucidate the point of the essay.
- setting up and knocking down a position: a position or claim believed by proponents of one side of a controversy, followed by statements that challenge that claim.
- historical perspective: an example of the way things used to be that leads into a discussion of how or why things work differently now.
- summary information: general introductory information about the topic that feeds into the essay's thesis statement.

Problem One
Reread the introductory paragraphs of the model essays and of the viewpoints in Section I. Identify which of the techniques described above are used in the example essays. How do they grab the attention of the reader? Are their thesis statements clearly presented?

Problem Two

Write an introduction for the essay you have outlined and partially written in Exercise 2B using one of the techniques described above.

The Conclusion

The conclusion brings the essay to a close by summarizing or returning to its main ideas. Good conclusions, however, go beyond simply repeating these ideas. Strong conclusions explore a topic's broader implications and reiterate why it is important to consider. They may frame the essay by returning to an anecdote featured in the opening paragraph. Or they may close with a quotation or refer back to an event in the essay. In opinionated essays, the conclusion can reiterate which side the essay is taking or ask the reader to reconsider a previously held position on the subject.

Problem Three

Reread the concluding paragraphs of the model essays and of the viewpoints in Section I. Which were most effective in driving their arguments home to the reader? What sorts of techniques did they use to do this? Did they appeal emotionally to the reader, or bookend an idea or event referenced elsewhere in the essay?

Problem Four

Write a conclusion for the essay you have outlined and partially written in Exercise 2B using one of the techniques described above.

Write Your Own Expository Five-Paragraph Essay

Using the information from this book, write your own five-paragraph expository essay on an issue relating to weapons of mass destruction. You can use the resources in this book for information about issues relating to this topic and how to structure this type of essay.

The following steps are suggestions on how to get started.

Step One: Choose your topic.

The first step is to decide what topic to write your expository essay on. Is there any subject that particularly fascinates you? Is there an issue you strongly support, or feel strongly against? Is there a topic you feel personally connected to or one that you would like to learn more about? Ask yourself such questions before selecting your essay topic. Refer to Appendix D: Sample Essay Topics if you need help selecting a topic.

Step Two: Write down questions and answers about the topic.

Before you begin writing, you will need to think carefully about what ideas your essay will contain. This is a process known as brainstorming. Brainstorming involves asking yourself questions and coming up with ideas to discuss in your essay. Possible questions that will help you with the brainstorming process include:

- Why is this topic important?
- Why should people be interested in this topic?
- How can I make this essay interesting to the reader?
- What question am I going to address in this paragraph or essay?
- What facts, ideas, or quotes can I use to support the answer to my question?

Questions especially for expository essays include:

- Do I want to write an informative essay or an opinionated essay?
- Will I need to explain a process or course of action?
- Will my essay contain many definitions or explanations?
- Is there a particular problem that needs to be solved?

Step Three: Gather facts, ideas, and anecdotes related to your topic.

This book contains several places to find information, including the viewpoints and the appendices. In addition, you may want to research the books, articles, and Web sites listed in Section III, or do additional research in your local library. You can also conduct interviews if you know someone who has a compelling story that would fit well in your essay.

Step Four: Develop a workable thesis statement.

Use what you have written down in steps two and three to help you articulate the main point or argument you want to make in your essay. It should be expressed in a clear sentence and make an arguable or supportable point.

Example:

The spread of weapons of mass destruction is one of the greatest threats facing the entire globe; leaders from all nations should therefore work together to make sure the world's most deadliest weapons are kept out of the hands of irresponsible governments.

(This could be the thesis statement of an expository essay that explains the importance of using diplomacy to curb the spread of weapons of mass destruction.)

Step Five: Write an outline or diagram.
- a. Write the thesis statement at the top of the outline.
- b. Write the roman numerals I, II, and III on the left side of the page.

    c. Next to each roman numeral, write down the best ideas you came up with in step three. These should all directly relate to and support the thesis statement.

    d. Next to each letter write down information that supports that particular idea.

Step Six: Write the three supporting paragraphs.

Use your outline to write the three supporting paragraphs. Write down the main idea of each paragraph in sentence form. Do the same thing for the supporting points of information. Each sentence should support the paragraph of the topic. Be sure you have relevant and interesting details, facts, and quotes. Use transitions when you move from idea to idea to keep the text fluid and smooth. Sometimes, although not always, paragraphs can include a concluding or summary sentence that restates the paragraph's argument.

Step Seven: Write the introduction and conclusion.

See Exercise 3B for information on writing introductions and conclusions.

Step Eight: Read and rewrite.

As you read, check your essay for the following:

✔ Does the essay maintain a consistent tone?

✔ Do all paragraphs reinforce your general thesis?

✔ Do all paragraphs flow from one to the other? Do you need to add transition words or phrases?

✔ Have you quoted from reliable, authoritative, and interesting sources?

✔ Is there a sense of progression throughout the essay?

✔ Does the essay get bogged down in too much detail or irrelevant material?

✔ Does your introduction grab the reader's attention?

✔ Does your conclusion reflect back on any previously discussed material, or give the essay a sense of closure?

✔ Are there any spelling or grammatical errors?

Section Three:
Supporting
Research
Material

Facts About Weapons of Mass Destruction

Editor's Note: These facts can be used in reports to reinforce or add credibility when making important points.

Historical Information about Weapons of Mass Destruction

- The term "weapons of mass destruction" was first used in a London Times article about the bombing of Spanish cities on December 28, 1937.
- The United Nations first used the term "weapons of mass destruction" in 1947, defining them as "atomic explosive weapons, radioactive material weapons, lethal chemical and biological weapons, and any weapons developed in the future which have characteristics comparable in destructive effect to those of the atomic bomb or other weapons mentioned above."
- In 2002, the Bush administration defined weapons of mass destruction as "nuclear, chemical, and biological weapons."
- The only nuclear weapons ever used in wartime were dropped on Japan by the U.S. at the end of WWII. The bomb dropped on the city of Hiroshima killed approximately 140,000 people; the bomb dropped on the city of Nagasaki killed approximately 70,000.
- The first nuclear weapons were called atom bombs, and averaged between 10–20 kilotons. The bomb dropped on the city of Hiroshima, for example, was around 15 kilotons, and the one on Nagasaki, about 21 kilotons.
- Modern nuclear weapons average more than 100 kilotons, with some as large as 300 kilotons.

Biological and Chemical Weapons

- Currently there are 16 states with chemical weapons programs, and 5–12 with biological weapons programs.
- Biological agents that can be weaponized include the following:
  - Anthrax—causes fever, cough, respiratory problems, and death
  - Botulism—causes weakness, dizziness, difficulty swallowing, blurred vision, paralysis, respiratory failure, and death
  - Bubonic Plague—causes high fever, blood poisoning, and death
  - Ricin—causes weakness, fever, cough, hypothermia, low blood pressure, heart failure, and death
  - Smallpox—causes fever, vomiting, headache, rash, bone marrow depression, bleeding, and death
- Chemical agents that can be weaponized include the following:
  - VX gas—causes difficulty breathing, vomiting, cramps, headache, confusion, convulsions, coma, and death
  - Mustard gas—causes blisters, vomiting, fever, blocks cell growth, and inflammation of respiratory organs
  - Sarin gas—cause bleeding from the nose and mouth, convulsions, coma, and death
- Since 1900, there have been 40 recorded bio-attacks, but many of them have been of minor significance.
- Since the 1980s there have been just 3 biochemical attacks; none of these has been very successful.
- One attack occurred in 1984, when a Hindu cult called Rajneeshee poisoned an Oregon salad bar with *Salmonella* bacteria. Seven hundred and fifty one people were sickened, but no one was killed.
- Another attack was perpetrated in 1995 by the Japanese terrorist group Aum Shinrikyo. The Japanese terrorists

released sarin gas on Tokyo subway system, killing 12 people and harming more than 50.

- In 2001, an anonymous terrorist or terrorist group sent anthrax-laced letters through the U.S. Postal Service, infecting 17 and killing five.
- Though each of these attacks frightened thousands, only 17 lives have been taken by biochemical terrorism in recent years.
- An example of a recent chemical weapons attack occurred in 1988, when former Iraqi dictator Saddam Hussein dropped bombs containing mustard gas, Sarin nerve gas and Tabun gas on the Kurdish city of Halabja. Estimates suggest that between 3,200 and 5,000 people were killed and many survivors suffered long-term health problems.

The Nuclear Non-Proliferation Treaty

- The Nuclear Non-Proliferation Treaty went into effect in 1970.
- It allows just five countries to have nuclear weapons (the five that possessed them at the time the Treaty was written): the United States, France, China, Great Britain, and the former Soviet Union (Russia).
- Since the NPT was established, four additional countries have acquired nuclear weapons—India (in 1974), Pakistan (in 1998), and North Korea (in 2006). Israel has not admitted to having nuclear weapons but it is widely believed that it does. India, Pakistan and Israel have never been signatories to the NPT.
- As of 2007, 189 countries have signed the Nuclear Non-Proliferation Treaty.
- Through the Nuclear Non-Proliferation Treaty, Belarus, Kazakhstan, Libya, South Africa, and the Ukraine have abandoned their nuclear weapons programs.
- Iran, Iraq and Libya violated the Nuclear Non-Proliferation Treaty by signing it and then continuing their WMD programs.

- North Korea was a signatory to the treaty, but withdrew in 2003 to pursue its nuclear weapons program over the objections of the international community. It consequently became a nuclear power in 2006.

Weapons of Mass Destruction around the World

- More than 128,000 nuclear warheads have been built worldwide since 1945.
- The total global nuclear weapons stockpile has been reduced from the 1986 Cold War high of 70,000-plus warheads to about 27,000 warheads, its lowest level in 45 years.
- 12,500 of these warheads are considered operational, with the rest in reserve or retired and awaiting dismantlement.
- There are nine nuclear weapon states—the United States, France, China, Great Britain, Russia, India, Pakistan, North Korea, and (unofficially) Israel.
- 97 percent of the world's nuclear weapons are in U.S. and Russian stockpiles.
- The U.S. has approximately 9,962 nuclear weapons, 5.735 of which are operational.
- Russia is estimated to have about 5,830 operational nuclear weapons.
- France has approximately 350 warheads.
- China is estimated to have a nuclear arsenal of about 200 nuclear warheads.
- Britain is estimated to have about 200 operational nuclear weapons.
- India and Pakistan have an estimated 110 nuclear warheads put together, but neither have released any official information to the public about the size of their arsenals.
- Israel is estimated to have between 60 and 85 warheads.

- North Korea is estimated to have between 6 and 10 nuclear weapons.
- After North Korea developed nuclear weapons, the UN adopted Resolution 1718, which imposed sanctions on the nation. Resolution 1718 banned the sale of luxury items to North Korea, which includes items such as automobiles, liquor, cigarettes melons, beef, and home electronic goods.
- The formerly-hostile nation of Libya was persuaded to dismantle its weapons of mass destruction programs on December 19, 2003. Libya was once regarded as a dangerous nation that supported terrorism, but the use of diplomacy eventually persuaded the regime it had more to gain without nuclear weapons than with them.

Nuclear Weapons and the United States

According to the Natural Resources Defense Council's Nuclear Notebook, the CIA, the Defense Intelligence Agency, and the Pentagon:

- As of 2006, the U.S. had a total of 9,962 nuclear weapons stationed in locations within the United States and around the world.
- This includes 5,735 active or operational warheads: 5,235 strategic and 500 non-strategic warheads.
- An estimated 4,225 additional warheads are held in reserve or inactive stockpiles, some of which will be dismantled.
- Approximately 4,365 warheads are scheduled to be retired for dismantlement by 2012.
- Since 1997, the Pentagon has removed nuclear weapons from three states (California, Virginia, and South Dakota).
- In 1991, the U.S. withdrew all of its nuclear weapons from South Korea and thousands more from Europe by 1993.

- It is estimated that as many as 400 nuclear bombs remain at eight facilities in six European countries, including Belgium, Germany, Italy, Netherlands, Turkey, and Britain.
- Nuclear warheads have been removed from Alaska, Canada, Chichi Jima, Cuba, France, Greece, Greenland, Guam, Hawaii, Iwo Jima, Japan, Johnston Island, Kwajalein Atoll, Midway Islands, Morocco, Okinawa, Philippines, Puerto Rico, South Korea, Spain, and Taiwan.
- Of the more than 70,000 warheads produced by the United States since 1945, more than 60,000 have been disassembled as of late 2006.
- The United States is responsible for building about 97 percent of the total nuclear weapons to ever have been built.

Opinions about Weapons of Mass Destruction and Terrorism

- According to a June 2006 *Los Angeles Times*/Bloomberg Poll, 56% of Americans believed Iran would acquire nuclear weapons despite diplomatic efforts or sanctions.
- According to a June 2006 CBS News Poll, 22 percent of Americans believed military action was the best way to deal with the threat from Iran, and believed that action should be taken soon.
- According to a May 2006 FOX News/Opinion Dynamics Poll, 74 percent believed the United Nations could not stop Iran from acquiring the technology to build weapons of mass destruction.
- According to a 2006 Foreign Policy poll of more than 100 experts and officials:
  - 47 percent viewed loose nuclear materials and weapons as the greatest threat to U.S. national security.

- 66 percent believed stopping the proliferation of nuclear weapons to rogue states should be a higher priority in fighting the war on terror.
- According to a September 2005 AP-Ipsos poll, 53 percent of Americans thought a nuclear attack by terrorists would be somewhat likely to occur within the U.S.
- According to a 2005 Zogby poll:
  - Just 39% of Americans said preparing for a nuclear attack should be the government's top focus.
  - Women appeared to be more concerned about the threat of a nuclear terrorist attack than men. 45% of women and 33% of men favored devoting resources to thwarting a nuclear terrorist attack.

Finding and Using Sources of Information

No matter what type of essay you are writing, it is necessary to find information to support your point of view. You can use sources such as books, magazine articles, newspaper articles, and online articles.

Using Books and Articles

You can find books and articles in a library by using the library's computer or cataloging system. If you are not sure how to use these resources, ask a librarian to help you. You can also use a computer to find many magazine articles and other articles written specifically for the Internet.

You are likely to find a lot more information than you can possibly use in your essay, so your first task is to narrow it down to what is likely to be most usable. Look at book and article titles. Look at book chapter titles, and examine the book's index to see if it contains information on the specific topic you want to write about. (For example, if you want to write about weaponized anthrax and you find a book about weapons of mass destruction, check the chapter titles and index to be sure it contains information relating to anthrax before you bother to check out the book.)

For a five-paragraph essay, you do not need a great deal of supporting information, so quickly try to narrow down your materials to a few good books and magazine or Internet articles. You do not need dozens. You might even find that one or two good books or articles contain all the information you need.

You probably do not have time to read an entire book, so find the chapters or sections that relate to your topic, and skim these. When you find useful information, copy it onto a note card or notebook. You should look for supporting facts, statistics, quotations, and examples.

Using the Internet

When you select your supporting information, it is important that you evaluate its source. This is especially important with information you find on the Internet. Because nearly anyone can put information on the Internet, there is as much bad information as good information. Before using Internet information—or any information—try to determine if the source seems to be reliable. Is the author or Internet site sponsored by a legitimate organization? Is it from a government source? Does the author have any special knowledge or training relating to the topic you are looking up? Does the article give any indication of where its information comes from?

Using Your Supporting Information

When you use supporting information from a book, article, interview or other source, there are three important things to remember:

1. *Make it clear whether you are using a direct quotation or a paraphrase.* If you copy information directly from your source, you are quoting it. You must put quotation marks around the information, and tell where the information comes from. If you put the information in your own words, you are paraphrasing it.

Here is an example of a using a quotation:

> Although many fear that terrorists might steal a nuclear weapon from an unguarded weapons facility, such a feat is not likely to be pulled off. In fact, "nuclear terrorism is not easy," writes one expert. "There are no known cases of theft or purchase of an intact nuclear weapon, so a terrorist attack with one is more than unlikely. There has not been any documented theft of enough fissile material for a crude nuke—although there have been attempts." (Rothstein et. al, 47)

Here is an example of a brief paraphrase of the same passage:

> Although many fear that terrorists might steal a nuclear weapon from an unguarded weapons facility, such a feat is not likely to be pulled off. In fact, experts such as Linda Rothstein, Catherine Auer, and Jonas Siegel cite the fact that there has never been a known theft of a nuclear weapon as proof that such a stunt is incredibly difficult to pull off. Although there have been attempts to steal such material, no one has ever succeeded—and it is likely that with the increased attention to this issue, stealing a nuclear weapon or materials will only become more difficult in the future.

2 *Use the information fairly.* Be careful to use supporting information in the way the author intended it. For example, it is unfair to quote an author as saying, "A nuclear terrorist attack is most definitely imminent" when he or she intended to say, "A nuclear terrorist attack is most definitely imminent—at least, this is what our politicians would like you to believe." This is called taking information out of context. This is using supporting evidence unfairly.

3. *Give credit where credit is due.* Giving credit is known as citing. You must use citations when you use someone else's information, but not every piece of supporting information needs a citation.

- If the supporting information is general knowledge—that is, it can be found in many sources—you do not have to cite your source.
- If you directly quote a source, you must cite it.
- If you paraphrase information from a specific source, you must cite it.

If you do not use citations where you should, you are plagiarizing—or stealing—someone else's work.

Citing Your Sources

There are a number of ways to cite your sources. Your teacher will probably want you to do it in one of three ways:

- Informal: As in the example in number 1 above, tell where you got the information as you present it in the text of your essay.
- Informal list: At the end of your essay, place an unnumbered list of all the sources you used. This tells the reader where, in general, your information came from.
- Formal: Use numbered footnotes. Footnotes are generally placed at the end of an article or essay, although they may be placed elsewhere depending on your teacher's requirements.

Works Cited

Rothstein, Linda, Catherine Auer, and Jonas Siegel. "Rethinking Doomsday." *Bulletin of the Atomic Scientists* Nov–Dec 2004: 47.

Using MLA Style to Create a Works Cited List

You will probably need to create a list of works cited for your paper. These include materials that you quoted from, relied heavily on, or consulted to write your paper. There are several different ways to structure these references. The following examples are based on Modern Language Association (MLA) style, one of the major citation styles used by writers.

Book Entries

For most book entries you will need the author's name, the book's title, where it was published, what company published it, and the year it was published. This information is usually found on the inside of the book. Variations on book entries include the following:

A Book by a Single Author
   Guest, Emma. *Children of AIDS: Africa's Orphan Crisis*. London: Sterling, 2003.

Two or More Books by the Same Author
   Friedman, Thomas L. *The World Is Flat: A Brief History of the Twentieth Century*. New York: Farrar, Straus and Giroux, 2005.

   ---. *From Beirut to Jerusalem*. New York: Doubleday, 1989.

A Book by Two or More Authors
   Pojman, Louis P., and Jeffrey Reiman. *The Death Penalty: For and Against*. Lanham, MD: Rowman & Littlefield, 1998.

A Book with an Editor
> Friedman, Lauri S., ed. *At Issue: What Motivates Suicide Bombers?* San Diego, CA: Greenhaven, 2004.

Periodical and Newspaper Entries

Entries for sources found in periodicals and newspapers are cited a bit differently than books. For one, these sources usually have a title and a publication name. They also may have specific dates and page numbers. Unlike book entries, you do not need to list where newspapers or periodicals are published or what company publishes them.

An Article from a Periodical
> Snow, Keith Harmon. "State Terror in Ethiopia." *Z Magazine* June 2004: 33–35.

An Unsigned Article from a Periodical
> "Broadcast Decency Rules." *Issues & Controversies on File* 30 Apr. 2004.

An Article from a Newspaper
> Constantino, Rebecca. "Fostering Love, Respecting Race." *Los Angeles Times* 14 Dec. 2002: B17.

Internet Sources

To document a source you found online, try to provide as much information on it as possible, including the author's name, the title of the document, date of publication or of last revision, the URL, and your date of access.

A Web Source

> Shyovitz, David. "The History and Development of Yiddish." Jewish Virtual Library. 30 May 2005 < http://www.jewishvirtuallibrary.org/jsource/History/yiddish.html. > . Accessed October 4, 2007.

Your teacher will tell you exactly how information should be cited in your essay. Generally, the very least information needed is the original author's name and the name of the article or other publication.

Be sure you know exactly what information your teacher requires before you start looking for your supporting information so that you know what information to include with your notes.

Sample Essay Topics

Persuasive Topics

The U.S. Is Likely to Be Attacked with Weapons of Mass Destruction

The U.S. Is Not Likely to Be Attacked with Weapons of Mass Destruction

Biological and Chemical Weapons Pose a Serious Threat

The Threat from Biological and Chemical Weapons is Exaggerated

Nuclear Weapons Pose a Serious Threat

The Threat from Nuclear Weapons has Been Exaggerated

Terrorists Are Likely to Steal Nuclear Materials or Weapons

Terrorists Are Not Likely to Steal Nuclear Materials or Weapons

Terrorists Are Likely to Make Their Own Weapons of Mass Destruction

Terrorists Are Not Likely to Make Their Own Weapons of Mass Destruction

The Spread of Weapons of Mass Destruction Can Be Prevented

Nothing Can Prevent the Spread of Weapons of Mass Destruction

The Nuclear Non-Proliferation Treaty Can Prevent the Spread of Weapons of Mass Destruction

The Nuclear Non-Proliferation Treaty Cannot Prevent the Spread of Weapons of Mass Destruction

International Cooperation Will Prevent the Spread of Weapons of Mass Destruction

America Should Give Up Its Nuclear Arsenal to Reduce the Spread of Weapons of Mass Destruction

American Should Not Give Up Its Nuclear Arsenal

Military Action Should Be Taken to Prevent Iran from Acquiring Weapons of Mass Destruction

Military Action Should Not Be Undertaken Against Iran

Sanctions Will Force North Korea to Give Up Its Weapons of Mass Destruction

Sanctions Will Not Force North Korea to Give Up Its Weapons of Mass Destruction

Diplomacy Will Force North Korea to Give Up Its Weapons of Mass Destruction

Bribery Will Force North Korea to Give Up Its Weapons of Mass Destruction

Expository Essay Topics

A History of Nuclear Weapons

A History of Biological and Chemical Weapons

How Biological and Chemical Weapons Work

The Devastating Power of a Nuclear Weapon

Cold War Bioweapons Programs and Their Legacy

Cold War Nuclear Weapons Programs and Their Legacy

How the Cold War Affected Today's WMD Problems

The Difference Between Peaceful and Hostile Nuclear Programs

Organizations to Contact

The American Civil Defense Association (TACDA)

11576 S. State St. Suite #502, Draper, UT 84020 • 800-425-5397 • e-mail: defense@tacda.org • Web site: www.tacda.org

TACDA promotes civil defense awareness and disaster preparedness, both in the military and private sector, and aims to assist citizens in their efforts to prepare for all types of natural and man-made disasters. Publications include the quarterly Journal of Civil Defense and the TACDA Alert newsletter.

American Enterprise Institute (AEI)

1150 Seventeenth St. NW, Washington, DC 20036 • (202) 862-5800: (202) 862-7177 • Web site: www.aei.org

The American Enterprise Institute for Public Policy Research is a scholarly research institute dedicated to preserving limited government, private enterprise, and a strong foreign policy and national defense.

America's Future

7800 Bonhomme Ave., St. Louis, MO 63105 • (314) 725-6003 • e-mail: info@americasfuture.net • Web site: http://www.americasfuture.net

America's Future supports continued U.S. testing of nuclear weapons and their usefulness as a deterrent of war. The group publishes the monthly newsletter *America's Future*.

Arms Control Association (ACA)

1150 Connecticut Avenue, NW, Suite 620, Washington, DC 20036 • (202) 463-8270 • e-mail: aca@armscontrol.org • Web site: http://www.armscontrol.org

The Arms Control Association believes the world should limit arms, reduce international tensions, and promote world peace. It publishes the monthly magazine *Arms Control Today* which frequently features articles about nuclear weapons.

Biohazard News (BHN)

925 Lakeville St.,P.O. Box 251, Petaluma, CA 94952 • e-mail: info@biohazardnews.net • Web site: www.biohazardnews.net/index.htm

BHN is a volunteer-run organization dedicated to providing the public timely information about the threat of biological terrorism, which it believes to be one of the most serious threats to America's national security. It publishes a free newsletter and maintains of website that includes interviews and information on biological weapons and terrorist groups.

Carnegie Endowment for International Peace

1779 Massachusetts Ave. NW, Washington, DC 20036 • (202) 483-7600 • e-mail: info@ceip.org • Web site: http://www.ceip.org

The Carnegie Endowment for International Peace conducts research on international affairs and U.S. foreign policy. Issues concerning nuclear weapons and proliferation are often discussed in articles published in its quarterly journal *Foreign Policy*.

Center for Defense Information (CDI)

1779 Massachusetts Ave. NW, Suite 615, Washington, DC 20036 • (202) 332-0600 • e-mail: info@cdi.org • Web site: http://www.cdi.org

CDI is comprised of civilians and former military officers who oppose both excessive expenditures for weapons and policies that increase the danger of war. The center monitors the military and analyzes spending, policies, weapon systems, and related military issues.

Center for Law and the Public's Health

Hampton House, Room 582, 624 North Broadway, Baltimore, MD 21205 • (410) 955-7624 • e-mail: jhodge@jhsph.edu • Web site: www.publichealthlaw.net

The center is a resource on practical and scholarly information on public health law. Reports and model legislation on legal issues related to biological warfare and terrorism can be found on its website.

Center for Nonproliferation Studies

460 Pierce Street, Monterey, CA 93940 • (831) 647-4154 • e-mail cns@miis.edu • Web site: http://cns.miis.edu

Researches all aspects of nonproliferation and works to combat the spread of weapons of mass destruction. Produces research databases and has multiple reports, papers, speeches, and congressional testimony available on-line. Its main publication is The Nonproliferation Review.

Center for Strategic and International Studies (CSIS)

1800 K St. NW, Suite 400, Washington, DC 20006 • (202) 887-0200 • fax: (202) 775-3199 • Web site: www.csis.org

The center works to provide world leaders with strategic insights and policy options on current and emerging global issues. It publishes books including *Combating Chemical, Biological, Radiological, and Nuclear Terrorism*, the *Washington Quarterly*, a journal on political, economic, and security issues, and other publications including reports that can be downloaded from its website.

Centers for Disease Control and Prevention
1600 Clifton Road, Atlanta, GA 30333 • (800) 311-3435 • e-mail: netinfo@cdc.gov • Web site: http://www.cdc.gov

The CDC is the government agency charged with protecting the public health of the nation by preventing and controlling diseases and by responding to public health emergencies. Programs of the CDC include the National Center for Infectious Diseases, which publishes the journal *Emerging Infectious Diseases*. Information on potential biological warfare agents, including anthrax and smallpox, is available on the CDC website.

Federation of American Scientists
1717 K. St., NW, Suite 209, Washington, DC 20036 • (202) 546-3300 • Web site: www.fas.org

The Federation of American Scientists was formed in 1945 by atomic scientists from the Manhattan Project who felt that scientists, engineers and other innovators had an ethical obligation to inform critical national pertaining to nuclear technology.

Food and Drug Administration
5600 Fishers Lane, Rockville, Maryland 20857 • (888) 463-6332 • Web site: www.fda.gov/oc/opacom/hottopics/bioterrorism.html

The FDA is a federal government public health agency that monitors the safety of the nation's foods and medicines. Its website includes a special section focusing on biological terrorism, including information on anthrax, how to handle suspicious letters, and food safety.

Henry L. Stimson Center

1111 19th Street Twelfth Floor, Washington, DC 20036 • (202) 223-5956 • e-mail: info@stimson.org • Web site: http://www.stimson.org

The Stimson Center directs the Chemical and Biological Weapons Nonproliferation Project, which produces papers, reports, handbooks, and books on chemical and biological weapon policy, nuclear policy, and eliminating weapons of mass destruction.

Johns Hopkins Center for Civilian Biodefense Strategies

111 Market Place, Suite 830, Baltimore, MD 21202 • (410) 223-1667 • fax: (410) 223-1665 • Web site: www. hopkins-biodefense.org/

The center is an independent, non-profit organization of the Johns Hopkins Bloomberg School of Public Health and the School of Medicine. It works to prevent the development and use of biological weapons and to advocate medical and public health policies that would minimize the damage of biological warfare. It does not provide clinical care or medical advice to individuals. It produces the journals *Biodefense Quarterly* and *Biosecurity and Bioterrorism*. Articles, reports, and other resources are available on its website.

Korean Peninsula Energy Development Organization (KEDO)

Public and External Promotion and Support Division, 600 Third Avenue, 12th Floor, New York, NY 10016 • (212) 455-0200 • Web site: www.kedo.org

KEDO is an international nonprofit organization established to carry out key provisions of the Agreed Framework negotiated in 1994 between the United States and North

Korea in which North Korea promised to freeze its nuclear facilities development. The organization works to help North Korea build civilian nuclear reactors and provide other energy sources to that nation.

Nuclear Age Peace Foundation

1187 Coast Village Road, Suite 1, PMB 121, Santa Barbara, California 93108-2794 • (805) 965-3443 • Web site: www.wagingpeace.org

The Nuclear Age Peace Foundation is a non-profit, non-partisan international education and advocacy organization, initiates and supports worldwide efforts to abolish nuclear weapons, to strengthen international law and institutions, to use technology responsibly, and to empower youth to create a more peaceful world.

Peace Action

1100 Wayne Ave. Suite 1020, Silver Spring, MD 20910 • (301) 565-4050 • e-mail: paprog@igc.org • Web site: www.peace-action.org

Peace Action is a grassroots peace and justice organization that works for policy changes on topics related to peace and disarmament issues. The organization produces a quarterly newsletter and also publishes an annual voting record for members of Congress.

Project Ploughshares

57 Erb Street West, Waterloo, Ontario, Canada N2L 6C2 (519) 888-6541 • e-mail: plough@ploughshares.ca • Web site: www.ploughshares.ca

Project Ploughshares promotes disarmament and demilitarization, the peaceful resolution of political conflict, and the pursuit of security based on equity, justice, and a sustainable environment.

Sunshine Project

101 West 6th Street, Suite 607, Austin, TX 78701 • (512) 494-0545 • e-mail: tsp@sunshine-project.org • Web site: www.sunshine-project.org

The Sunshine Project is an international non-governmental organization that works to avert the dangers of new weapons stemming from advances in biotechnology. It conducts research and issues reports on biological weapons research in Germany, the United States, and other countries. These reports and other information on biological weapons can be downloaded from its website.

Union of Concerned Scientists (UCS)

2 Brattle Sq., Cambridge, MA 02238(617) 547-5552 • fax: (617) 864-9405 • e-mail: ucs@ucsusa.org • Web site: www.ucsusa.org

UCS is concerned about the impact of advanced technology on society. It supports nuclear arms control as a means to reduce nuclear weapons. Publications include the quarterly *Nucleus* newsletter and reports and briefs concerning nuclear proliferation.

United States Arms Control and Disarmament Agency (ACDA)

320 21st St. NW, Washington, DC 20451 • phone: (800) 581-ACDA • Web site: http://dosfan.lib.uic.edu/acda/

The mission of the ACDA is to strengthen the national security of the United States by formulating, advocating, negotiating, implementing, and verifying effective arms control, nonproliferation, and disarmament policies, strategies, and agreements. The agency publishes fact sheets on the disarmament of weapons of mass destruction as well as on-line records of speeches, treaties, and reports related to arms control.

U.S. Department of State, Bureau of Nonproliferation

Public Communications Division, 2201 C St. NW, Washington, DC 20520 • (202) 647-6575 • Web site: www.state.gov/t/isn/

The Bureau of Nonproliferation leads U.S. efforts to prevent the spread of weapons of mass destruction, including biological weapons. The Bureau has primary responsibility for leadership in the interagency process for nonproliferation issues; leads major nonproliferation negotiations and discussions with other countries; and participates in all nonproliferation-related dialogues. Its website offers speeches and news briefings on U.S. foreign policy related to biological weapons.

Bibliography

Books

Kaveh L. Afrasiabi, *Iran's Nuclear Program: Debating Facts Versus Fiction*. Charleston, SC: BookSurge Publishing, 2006.

Graham Allison, *Nuclear Terrorism: The Ultimate Preventable Catastrophe*. New York: Henry Holt, 2004.

Kurt M. Campbell, Robert J. Einhorn, Mitchell B. Reiss, eds., *The Nuclear Tipping Point: Why States Reconsider Their Nuclear Choices*. Washington DC: Brookings Institution Press, 2004.

Victor D. Cha and David C. Kang, *Nuclear North Korea: A Debate on Engagement Strategies*. New York: Columbia University Press, 2005.

Gordon G. Chang, *Nuclear Showdown: North Korea Takes On the World*. New York: Random House, 2006.

Joseph Cirincione, Jon B. Wolfsthal, and Miriam Rajkumar, *Deadly Arsenals: Nuclear, Biological and Chemical Threats*, Washington DC: Carnegie Endowment for International Peace, 2005.

Clark Kent Ervin, *Open Target: Where America Is Vulnerable to Attack*. New York: Palgrave MacMillan, 2006.

Michael D. Evans and Jerome R. Corsi, *Showdown with Nuclear Iran: Radical Islam's Messianic Mission to Destroy Israel and Cripple the United States*. Nashville, TN: Nelson Current, 2006.

Mark Hitchcock, *Iran: The Coming Crisis: Radical Islam, Oil, and the Nuclear Threat*. Sisters, OR: Multnomah, 2006.

Al Mauroni, *Chemical and Biological Warfare*, Santa Barbara, CA: ABC-CLIO, 2006.

Nick McCamley, *Secret Biological Warfare*, London: Pen and Sword, 2007.

Gavan McCormack, *Target North Korea: Pushing North Korea to the Brink of Nuclear Catastrophe*. New York: Nation Books, 2004.

Michael O'Hanlon, Mike M. Mochizuki, *Crisis on the Korean Peninsula: How to Deal With a Nuclear North Korea*. New York: McGraw-Hill, 2003.

Barry R. Schneider, ed. *Avoiding the Abyss: Progress, Shortfalls, and the Way Ahead in Combating the WMD Threat*. Westport, CT: Praeger Security International, 2006.

Kenneth R. Timmerman, *Countdown to Crisis: The Coming Nuclear Showdown with Iran*. New York: Crown Publishing Group, 2006.

Al Venter, *Iran's Nuclear Option: Tehran's Quest for the Atom Bomb*. Drexel Hill, PA: Casemate, 2005.

Norbert Vollertsen, *Inside North Korea*. New York: Encounter Books, 2006.

Periodicals

"How Safe a World?" *Boston Globe*, September 11, 2006, p. A 10.

Steve Andreasen and Dennis Gormley, "Edging Ever Closer to a Nuclear Death," *Minneapolis Star Tribune*, March 29, 2006.

William M. Arkin, "The Continuing Misuses of Fear," *Bulletin of the Atomic Scientists*, Vol. 62, No. 5, Sep–Oct 2006, p. 42–45.

Reza Aslan, "Misunderstanding Iran" *The Nation* 280.8 (Feb 28, 2005): p26.

Gawdat Bahgat, "Nonproliferation Success: The Libyan Model," *World Affairs*, Summer 2005, Vol 168, Issue 1, p. 3.

Dorothy Boulware, "Is the USA Ready for War at Home?" *Afro-American,* Jul 29–Aug 4, 2006, p. A10.

George W. Bush, "Remarks by the President on Weapons of Mass Destruction Proliferation," February 11, 2004. www.whitehouse.gov/news/releases/2004/02/print/20040211-4.html

George Bunn, "Enforcing International Standards: Protecting Nuclear Materials from Terrorists Post-9/11," *Arms Control Today,* Jan–Feb 2007, p. 14.

Patrick Briley, "Hezbollah, WMD Attacks, Inside U.S. Cities?" *NewsWithViews.com,* February 10, 2006. www.newswithviews.com/Briley/Patrick22.htm

Ted Galen Carpenter, "Iran's Nuclear Program, America's Policy Options," Cato Institute Policy Analysis No. 578, September 20, 2006.

Nigel Chamberlain, "Nuclear Deterrence," British American Security Information Council, July 20, 2006. www.basicint.org/pubs/Notes/BN060720.htm

Leonard A. Cole, "Bioweapons, Proliferation, and the U.S. Anthrax Attack," Center for Contemporary Conflict, http://www.ccc.nps.navy.mil//events/recent/Presentations/Cole%20Bio%20paper.pdf.

David Cortright, "The New Nuclear Danger: A Strategy of Selective Coercion is Fundamentally Flawed," *America,* December 11, 2006, p. 18.

Veronique de Rugy, "Is Port Security Spending Making Us Safer?" American Enterprise

Institute. Working Paper #115. Sept. 7, 2005. p. 8.

Daniel Doron, "Yes, Iran Can Be Stopped," *Weekly Standard,* February 1, 2007.

Michael Duffy, "What Would War Look Like?" *Time,* September 25, 2006.

Gwynne Dyer, "Why Not Offer Kim Jong-Il Something of Value to Head off a Nuclear Crisis?" *Athens News* (Athens, OH), October 12, 2006.

M.M. Eskandari-Qajar, "All Talk, No Nukes," *Santa Barbara Independent*, Vol. 20, Issue 2, Jan 26–Feb 2, 2006, p. 11.

Stephan Faris, "Containment Strategy," *Atlantic Monthly*, December 2006, p. 34.

Trevor Findlay, "Why treaties work or don't work," *Behind the Headlines*, Autumn 2005, p. 1.

Norman Friedman, "The Case for Pre-Emption," United States Naval Institute, Proceedings, Vol. 132, Iss. 8, p. 90.

Bill Frist, "Remarks to the World Economic Forum in Davos, Switzerland," January 27, 2005. http://www.zkea.com/news_archive.html?ARCHIVE = 05-01-31

Robert L. Gallucci, "Let's Make a Deal," *Time*, October 23, 2006, p. 38.

James Goodby, "U.S. Must Take Offensive Against Nuclear Terrorism," *Baltimore Sun*, February 4, 2007, p. A23.

Dennis M. Gormley, "Securing Nuclear Obsolescence," *Survival*, Vol. 48, No. 3., Autumn 2006, p. 127–148.

Robert E. Hunter, "The Iran Case: Addressing Why Countries Want Nuclear Weapons," *Arms Control Today*, December 2004, p. 22.

David Isenberg, "See, Speak, and Hear No Incompetence," British American Security Information Council, October, 2005. www.basicint.org/pubs/Research/05WMD.pdf

Han Sung Joo, "Better Than Nothing," *Time International*, February 26, 2007, p. 23.

Liaquat Ali Khan, "Nuclear Non-Proliferation Treaty Poised to Fall Apart," *Counterpunch.org*, May 4, 2005.

Nicholas D. Kristoff, "Send in the Fat Guys," *New York Times*, October 22, 2006, p. 4.

William Kristol, "And Now Iran; We Can't Rule Out the Use of Military Force," *Weekly Standard*, January 23, 2006.

William Langewiesche, "Living with the Bomb," *Los Angeles Times,* October 15, 2006, p. M1.

Milton Leitenberg, "Assessing the Biological Weapons and Bioterrorism Threat," Strategic Studies Institute, December 005. http://www.terrorisminfo.mipt.org/pdf/Assessing-Biological-Weapons-Bioterrorism-Threat.pdf

Anatol Lieven and John Hulsman, "North Korea's Not Our Problem," *Los Angeles Times,* October 11, 2006, p. B13.

Allison Macfarlane, "All Weapons of Mass Destruction Are Not Equal," *Alternet,* February 8, 2006. www.alternet.org/story/31510

Angie C. Marek, "A Nuclear Headache," *U.S. News & World Report,* February 26, 2007, p. 27–28.

Judith Miller, "Gadhafi's Leap of Faith," *Wall Street Journal,* May 17, 2006, p. A18.

John Mueller, "A False Sense of Insecurity?" *Regulation,* Fall 2004.

Joseph C. Myers, "Why We Can't Deter Iran (Because We Aren't)" *American Thinker,* June 6, 2006.

William Perry, "Post-Cold War U. S. Nuclear Strategy: A Search for Technical and Policy Common Ground," Remarks to the National Academy of Sciences, August 11, 2004.

Stephen G. Rademaker, U.S. Statement at the 2005 Nuclear Non-Proliferation Treaty Review Conference, May 2, 2005. www.state.gov/t/ac/rls/rm/45518.htm.

Susan E. Rice, "We Need to Talk to North Korea," *Washington Post,* June 3, 2005.

Noah Shachtman, "Bigger Worries than BioChem," *TCSDaily,* October 8, 2003.

Pandy R. Sinish and Joel A. Vilensky, "WMDs in our backyards," *Earth Island Journal* 19.4 (Wntr 2005): p31(4).

George Tenet, "Written Statement for the Record of the Director of Central Intelligence Before the National Commission on Terrorist Attacks Upon the United States," March 24, 2002, p. 32.

Fareed Zakaria, "Let Them Eat Carrots," *Newsweek,* October 23, 2006, p. 42.

Mark Williams, "The Knowledge," *Technology Review,* March/April 2006.

Heather Wokusch, "Who's the Real WMD Threat? How the Bush Administration's Biological Weapons Buildup Affects You" *Antiwar.Com,* April 15, 2005. http://www.antiwar.com/orig/wokusch.php?articleid = 5564

Web Sites

ACP-ASIM Online Bioterrorism Resources (www.acponline.org/bioterro/index.html). The American College of Physicians-American Society of Internal Medicine (ACP-ASIM) is the nation's largest medical specialty society. Its Bioterrorism Resources webpage includes medical information on anthrax, smallpox, and other biological agents.

All the Virology on the WWW (www.virology.net/garryfavwebbw.html). All the Virology on the WWW is the leading Internet site for information on viruses. It includes a special section on biological warfare.

Anthrax Vaccine Immunization Program (www.anthrax.osd.mil/). The official U.S. Department of Defense anthrax information website provides news and documents related to anthrax and the military vaccination programs.

Defense Threat Reduction Agency (www.dtra.mil). Part of the U.S. Department of Defense, this agency manages America's chemical and biological defense efforts. The website contains information on their programs and initiatives.

Public Health Emergency Preparedness and Response (www.bt.cdc.gov). The Centers for Disease Control and Prevention's main site for information on biological, chemical, and radiological threats. Resources include fact sheets, news briefs, and emergency response guidelines.

The Non-Proliferation Project (www.carnegieendowment.org/npp/). The Carnegie Endowment for International Peace offers an arsenal of information on WMD. Find expert analysis of the WMD capabilities of countries around the world, and charts, reports, and Congressional testimony on nuclear, chemical, and biological weapons and treaties.

Downwinders (www.downwinders.org). Read about the dangers of fallout from nuclear testing, efforts to compensate victims of radiation exposure, and the future of nuclear testing in the U.S.

Index

Picture Credits

About the Editor

Lauri S. Friedman earned her bachelor's degree in religion and political science from Vassar College in Poughkeepsie, NY. Her studies there focused on political Islam. Friedman has worked as a non-fiction writer, a newspaper journalist, and an editor for more than 7 years. She has accumulated extensive experience in both academic and professional settings.

Friedman has edited and authored numerous publications for Greenhaven Press on controversial social issues such as gay marriage, Islam, energy, discrimination, suicide bombers, and the war on terror. Much of the *Writing the Critical Essay* series has been under her direction or authorship. She was instrumental in the creation of the series, and played a critical role in its conception and development.